FORAGING MUSHROOMS
WASHINGTON

FORAGING MUSHROOMS WASHINGTON

Finding, Identifying, and Preparing
Edible Wild Mushrooms

Jim Meuninck

GUILFORD, CONNECTICUT

FALCONGUIDES®

An imprint of The Rowman & Littlefield Publishing Group, Inc.
4501 Forbes Blvd., Ste. 200
Lanham, MD 20706
www.rowman.com

Falcon and FalconGuides are registered trademarks and Make Adventure Your Story is a trademark of The Rowman & Littlefield Publishing Group, Inc.

Distributed by NATIONAL BOOK NETWORK

Photos by Jim Meuninck unless otherwise noted.

Map by The Rowman & Littlefield Publishing Group, Inc.

British Library Cataloguing-in-Publication Information Available

Library of Congress Cataloging in Publication Data available

ISBN 978-1-4930-3642-4 (hardcover/paperback)
ISBN 978-1-4930-3643-1 (e-book)

∞™ The paper used in this publication meets the minimum requirements of American National Standard for Information Sciences—Permanence of Paper for Printed Library Materials, ANSI/NISO Z39.48-1992.

Printed in the United States of America

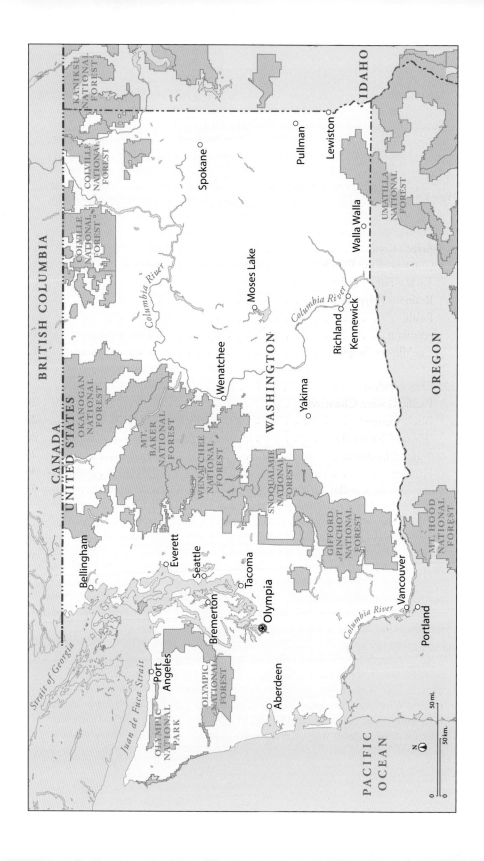

CONTENTS

ACKNOWLEDGMENTS

In my short time canvassing Earth, I have been fortunate to meet and work with caring human beings who love the planet and appreciate the profound experience they have inherited. Here are a few cheers for the writers and explorers who made this book possible. Thank you Hugh Smith for the terrific photos that improve the usefulness of this field guide. Thank you for your love of life and dedication to discovery. Hugh and Sandi, his spouse, have discovered and placed mushroom photos everywhere on the internet for us to enjoy. Making their acquaintance has greatly enhanced my mushroom field experiences. They made this book possible. Of course, the biggest place in my heart is reserved for Jill, my spouse and inspiration. Jill's extraordinary vision finds what we are looking for from the truck window, 50 yards deep in the forest, as we pass by at 60 miles per hour. These special sorties into wilderness with Jill are not possible without the guidance of the entire FalconGuide staff and my editors David Legere, Karen Ackerman, and Kristen Mellitt, who helped me along the path to completion. Editors, proofreaders, layout, and design troops make all the difference between ordinary and excellent. Thank you all.

And thanks to you, the forager, for picking up this book and taking it afield. I hope you are searching in deep solitude, surrounded by big trees, moving along, stop and go, at a half mile per hour, finding mushrooms. If so, mission accomplished.

INTRODUCTION

Washington State provides the knowledgeable wilderness traveler with a staggering supply of free groceries: fruit, nuts, wild edibles, and mushrooms. The goal of this entry-level field guide is to help foragers, homemakers, health practitioners, nutritionists, and chefs choose wisely from fifty different edible Washington mushrooms. To make this experience safe and easy, the first eight chapters of this field guide to edible Washington mushrooms identifies fairly simple-to-identify edible mushrooms. The first chapters hone skills and build your repertoire with familiar mushrooms like polypores, chanterelles, boletes, tooth fungi, puffballs, and morels. And here is the bonus: Science strongly suggests that adding mushrooms to a broad-based holistic diet provides nutritional benefits with a health-protecting boost. Present to your palate these rewarding and sustaining field and forest creatures that make a good life even better.

Permits and Collection Limits

Collection limits and permits are enforced within Washington State. Be certain to know what limitations and/or permits are necessary (if any) for a particular state park, city park, national park, or national forest area. Native American land may also require permission and permits and have limits. Fines may be excessive. A useful collection of rules and permits may be downloaded at www.psms.org/WAMushroomRulesMay2016.pdf.

Staying Found

Someone loves you, and others do not want to have to search for you, so carry a compass and/or a GPS navigation device when mushroom foraging in big country. Orient your starting position with the road, the sun, and landmarks such as a mountain or river. I prefer hunting along a stream that crosses the road where I have parked. Keeping the stream in sight while foraging provides a sure route back to your vehicle. Mushrooms love stream banks and aprons—streamsides and their tributaries provide opportunity.

Logging trails and animal trails are also useful. Arrange sticks or stones on these trails pointing your way back to the road, especially where trails intersect and where you change direction.

When there are no trails or streams, hunt uphill or downhill from the road or trail. Take a compass reading and then head either up or down, remembering that you must reverse the direction upon your return. There is no guarantee you will get back to where you started, but there is a good chance you will arrive back at the road by using this method.

If you forage in wilderness, consider a Personal Location Beacon device. They work off satellites and may be purchased for your next mushroom sortie into big country. See reviews of the technology at www.rei.com/learn/expert-advice/personal-locator-beacons.html. Always tell someone where you are hunting and beware of logging trucks and hunters.

WHERE IN WASHINGTON

You will find mushrooms in coastal forests, dune areas, cow pastures, mountainous old growths, reservations, national parks, your backyard, the city park, neighborhood streets, along streams and rivers, and in rain forests.

In April begin morel hunting along mountain flanks, valley floors, in hardwood and conifer forests, campground edges, conifer forest burns, and pear and apple orchards. The morel season is extended as you climb higher, and these mushrooms can be found as late as August.

West of the Olympics near Neah Bay on the Makah Indian Reservation, there are numerous species found along the Cape Flattery walk to the farthest western point in the lower forty-eight. The constant mist from the Pacific on the cape provides mushrooms in every month. From there travel from Neah Bay to Lake Ozette, where the campground and surrounding forest give up angel wings and oyster mushrooms among others. Continuing south on US 101 along the coast near Kalaloch, side roads are productive in all seasons thanks to the ocean's fog and drizzle. Olympic National Park has numerous roads that take you to mushrooms, although they're not productive in the dry summer months. September, October, and November are best. Try the west side of Quinault beyond the lake of the same name. Mushrooms are along the road and up the trails in late summer and fall. The Hoh Rain Forest is a good bet in the same time period. Also, look near Hurricane Ridge and down the east side of the park at Duckabush and Brinnon. Trails deeper into the Olympics are mushroom-heavy in the wet season.

Back on 101, moving down toward the Columbia River, there are a couple more mushroom haunts along the ocean near Ocean City, Grayland, Ocean Park, and Long Beach. Work in and around the campgrounds and along the dunes and beaches. The Columbia River Gorge heading west along WA 14 is a bit dismal for mushroom hunting on the river side, but it's much better in the mountains north of the road. The Mount St. Helens area and Mount Adams are great. Find chanterelles, *Laetiporus*, puffballs, morels, and more in season. The Sunrise entrance to Mount Rainier is good with a wide variety of toothed fungus, polypores, and corals. Rainier and its many campgrounds are a mushroom forager's dream or nightmare—have several field guides to alleviate your frustration.

The Darrington Mountain Loop Highway has striking terrain and ocean-facing mountains presenting numerous varieties of mushrooms in all seasons. See ling chi on the trail to the Ice Caves. Then, north and west of Darrington are the Mount Baker Wilderness and the North Cascades. Here, in the cooler months, find American matsutake and chanterelles as well as boletes, edible mycenas, and toothed fungi to name a few. Work the drier east side of the Cascades as wet weather permits, and the wetter west side earlier and often.

WA 20 provides access to the Pacific Crest Trail, a challenging trek with streams and rivers to encourage fungi dispersal. Had enough remote trekking? Then head to the northeast and southeast corners where in the spring morels are found in April and May and later at higher latitudes. Try old pear orchards, burnouts, city and county parks, as well as trail edges and roadsides. Morels are found throughout the state. And don't forget that campground trails and hiking trails provide access, so use them. Heliotrope Trail toward Mount Baker will make you happy and mushroom-rich.

TIPS: FROM THE FIELD TO THE KITCHEN

Gathering: Collect mushrooms in a basket or mesh bag so spores may be returned to the earth as you walk.

Cleaning: If mushrooms are wet, pat them dry before storing. Do not wash before storing. Brush or wipe or store as is from the forest.

Fresh storage: Store in a closed paper bag or wrap in a damp cloth—damp, not wet. Fresh mushrooms will keep for a week in a cold refrigerator. Keep the temperature between 32 and 36 degrees F. Do not store fresh mushrooms in a plastic bag.

Drying: Use a food dryer or an oven with the door ajar. Drying in the sun increases vitamin D in mushrooms. Dry them for a while outdoors on a sunny day and finish in the oven or electric dryer. Keep the temperature between 130 and 140 degrees F. Dry until mushrooms are tortilla-chip crisp. Place dried mushrooms in a locking plastic bag and/or stuff in a sealed container. Keep the mushrooms out of direct light as much as possible. Bone-dry mushrooms, adequately sealed, will hold for a year. For several more ways to dry mushrooms see www.wikihow.com/dry-mushrooms.

Freezing: Freeze mushrooms fresh from the forest or in cooked dishes. If frozen raw, consume in four weeks or less. Frozen dishes are good for up to one year. Oyster mushrooms can be parboiled or steamed and then frozen.

Cooking: Place the frozen mushroom directly into a *hot* cooking dish or sautéing pan. This procedure protects the texture and integrity of the mushroom. Dried mushrooms may be cooked without rehydration, especially if their flesh is thin. Throw them in the pan and they will take moisture from whatever else you are cooking them with and impart their flavor to the same. There are numerous recipes throughout this book.

HOW TO USE THIS GUIDE

The organization of this field guide makes it an effective tool. Both the common names and the binomial genus species names are used. This guide breaks down each entry by **Common name(s)**, **Family** name, and binomial name, **Origin** of the name, **Season, Identification, Spore ID, Habitat, Look-alikes, Edibility, Medicinal Uses, Storage** tips (for example, always cook a frozen mushroom while still frozen to avoid softening), author's **Comments**, and a **Recipe**. Appendices include **recipe resources**, a **grow your own mushrooms** section, **recommended books**, and more. Finally, there is a **bibliography** and an index.

Eight Mushroom-Gathering Strategies

To identify a mushroom, follow this advice:

1. **Use field guides:** I have fourteen field guides and typically cross-reference a new mushroom in as many of them as time and endurance allow.
2. **Join a mushroom society or club:** This will shortcut your way to success. Clubs help you find like-minded friends and uncover ground where you never thought to look. They quickly add to your repertoire of known mushrooms.
3. **Get field experience:** Travel by foot and observe the characteristics of the many different mushroom environments. Do this often. Discover where the remaining old-growth forests are in your area and visit them. Understand that in newly planted forests (say, after a forest fire), both hardwoods and conifers provide super resources for newly developing saprophytic mushrooms. Frequent visits to a variety of forest and field biomes will, over the four seasons, reward you with the right places to go.
4. **Discover mushroom partners:** Mushrooms, animals, and plants live in close relationship with one another. You'll find oyster mushrooms on maple and alder and less commonly on conifers. Locate morels in association with old apple and pear orchards. Seek them in recently burned-out conifer forests. These relationships are attended to in the text of each species, and identifying various Washington trees associated with mushrooms is covered in the next section following these strategies.
5. **Identify mushroom structure:** Mushrooms have a cap (pileous), stems (stipes), rings (annulus), and veils. Spores are reproduction bodies and come in various sizes, colors, and shapes. Spore-producing and disseminating organs are teeth, pores, gills, and in puffballs the entire inner area of the mushroom. A mushroom may have scales, hair, warts, scabs, and striations—or it may be smooth. Many mushrooms have a volva (an egg-like

sack) from which they emerge. They may have rings, hanging remnants of a veil that covered the gills. In addition, mushroom structures come in numerous colors. A few mushrooms present juices or may bruise into different colors when handled. They are dry and smooth or moist and slippery, and a few have dots or are reticulated. Different species may be hard, fragile, flexible, or brittle. They have distinctive odors and distinctive flavors.

6. **Make spore prints:** Use spores as an identification tool: Separate the cap of a mushroom from its stem, and place it over the intersection of two pieces of paper (or other two-dimensional surface), one piece white and the other black. Clear glass is a particularly effective material. A spore print on glass allows you to scrape spores onto a microscope slide without contamination. It also allows you to scrape large numbers of spores for inoculation when growing your own mushrooms (see appendix B). After a few minutes or several hours, spores will drop from the mushroom's gills, pores, or teeth, leaving a spore print. The color of this print helps indicate the mushroom's identity.

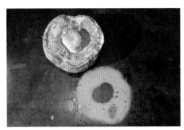

Boletales spore print

Gymnopilus spore print

7. **Learn about chemical tests and microscopy:** This requires a basic knowledge of chemistry, safe handling, and access. Chemicals used include ammonia (NH4OH ammonium hydroxide), potassium hydroxide (KOH), iron salts (FeSO4), concentrated hydrochloric acid (HCl), and Melzer's reagent (iodine, methyl chloride, and potassium iodide). For the mushrooms identified in this book, these tests are not absolutely necessary. However, should you go beyond the basics, familiarize yourself with chemical testing at these websites:

    Using potassium hydroxide: www.mushroomexpert.com/microscope_ascos.html

    Using Mezger's reagent: www.mushroomexpert.com/microscope_spores.html

    Microscope and reagent use: www.first-nature.com/fungi/facts/microscopy.php

    www.centralpamushroomclub.org/sites/default/files/melzer.pdf

    http://en.wikipedia.org/wiki/Melzer's_reagent

    Surfaces and flesh testing: www.mushroomexpert.com/macrochemicals.html

Overview: http://en.wikipedia.org/wiki/Chemical_tests_in_mushroom
_identification

8. **Forage familiar ground:** As you expand your knowledge, you will discover forests and fields that provide what you are looking for when you are looking for it and often reward you with a new find. Note these places in your mushroom notebook. Cherish and visit them often. These secret sanctuaries provide all the clues and context needed to be successful. Old-growth forests are most productive. After a few trips you will have a mental map and cognitive timetable that will lead you to a specific site at the right time of year to find exactly what you want.

Simplifying the Fungisphere

This guide starts with easier-to-identify mushrooms and progresses to mushrooms that are more difficult to identify. For example, the first broad group of mushrooms a forager encounters in these pages are polypores with spore-emitting pores. Then comes tooth fungi with spore-producing spines or teeth. Chanterelles follow, with their ridges instead of gills. These ridges, unlike gills, are folds integrated with and part of the fruiting body's flesh. Boletes come after chanterelles, and they produce and emit spores from tubes, whereas next, the puffballs, produce spores within their ball-like bodies and then emit them through a vent. You will experience these simpler-to-identify mushrooms in the field or you may purchase them from a farmer's market.

There are a few pitfalls when searching for specific species and I will help you identify them. Following mushrooms with tubes, pores, ridges, teeth, and spherical puffballs are morels, with unique structures of their own. All of these can be found in the field or in the market. Coral mushrooms and gelatinous mushrooms follow the morels, and they are fairly easy to identify because of their atypical physical qualities. Eventually, you will reach a few families of gilled mushrooms, a vast group that includes many toxic varieties that require rigorous identification and cautious respect. This large group of gilled mushrooms is comprised of both delicious and toxic species. The final two chapters cover commercially available mushrooms and a few of the many difficult-to-identify and potentially toxic mushrooms. Throughout the book I will share tips for identifying, preparing, preserving, and growing your own mushrooms. All of this information is supported with mushroom-related websites and recipe resources that will delight your family and friends.

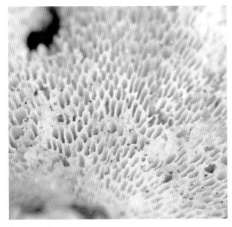

Pores, polypore

Tubes, bolete

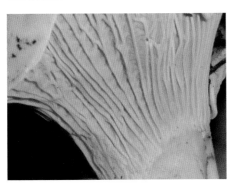

Integrated ridges, chanterelle

Teeth, lion's mane

Gills, *Marasmius*

WASHINGTON TREES AND ASSOCIATED MUSHROOMS

A successful search for mushrooms improves when you know the habitat in which they reside and the trees and other flora associated with them. Below are photos of trees that have relationships with specific fungi. For example, in the young, densely replanted forests of western hemlock and Douglas fir, chanterelles are found in abundance. Find cauliflower fungus on mature Douglas firs. Morels and king boletes are found in burned-out and recovering areas of lodgepole pine, larch, white fir, and Douglas fir. Oyster mushrooms are found on cottonwood, poplar, birch, maple, and alder. Look for matsutakes in association with western hemlock, sitka spruce, and pine trees. It is hypothesized that potent psilocybes are found in conjunction with alder and/or animal feces. Found in association with madrone are *Leccinum*, *Mycenas*, *Tricholomas*, and *Amanitas* species to name a few. Honey mushrooms, *Trametes*, and a number of polypores are found on or in association with big-leaf maple trees. Ponderosa pine habitats may produce *Armillaria* (honey mushrooms), matsutakes, boletes, *Suillus*, slippery jacks, and Amanitas. When foraging for mushrooms take notes and write down the trees that surround your find, and your futures sorties will become more productive.

Western hemlock (*Tsuga heterophylla*) has cones 1 inch long and often found in abundance under the tree. Young trees have drooping tops. The needles are soft and whitish underneath.

Douglas fir (*Pseudotsuga menzies*) has pinecones up to 4 inches long, and if you look closely you will see what can be imagined as the hind legs and tails of mice ducked into the cone. The bark of a mature tree is deeply furrowed and thick (fire resistant).

Spruce (*Picea*) has sharp and stiff needles that are painful to grasp. Cones are up to 3 inches long and soft and papery to the touch. Bark has a chip appearance and is thin and scaly looking.

Cedar (*Thuja plicata*) is little mentioned in association with mushrooms because of its acidic nature and associated fungicides in its chemistry. It has small, flat, scaly leaves, branches that hang like fronds, and half-inch-long cones.

Red alder (*Alnus rubra*) is a deciduous tree, shedding leaves in the fall. It is similar to birch but has rougher leaves, and the whitish color of alder is caused by lichens living under the bark.

Big-leaf maple (*Acer macrophyllum*) is a large maple with five lobed leaves, 5 to 12 inches long, as wide as they are long. These trees are richly adorned with lichens, ferns, club mosses, and true mosses that do not harm the tree and take their nutrients from the air.

Madrone is a Pacific Coast dweller and offers mushroom-foraging opportunities. Its bark is striking and unique.

Larch trees are also good places to find specific mushrooms such as agarikon and *Laetiporus conifericola*. They thrive near water and have unique needles and cones.

Ponderosa pine has unique bark. Mature trees have yellow to orange and red bark displayed in broad plates separated by black crevices. Younger trees have blackish-brown bark. There are five subspecies. Needles are long and bright green.

1   Polypores

Pores of a polypore

Origin: Greek/Latin meaning "many pores"

Polypore mushrooms are typically the first mushrooms you see in a forest, and you see them everywhere growing on trees, twigs, stumps, and roots. They are visible year-round so it is logical to start with this prolific and very visible family.

Polypores produce and distribute spores from tubes through pores. They are the most conspicuous mushrooms in Washington, seen year-round. A few are edible and others may be prepared as health-protecting teas, drinks, and soups. They are parasitic or saprophytic or both, and are typically shelf or hoof-shaped mushrooms (but not always). Find them clinging to trees across the continent. Here are some of the most important edible and/or medicinal polypore mushrooms found in Washington, especially in rare old-growth forests. Because these mushrooms may be inedible due to their hardness, there is a Health Prep section describing the various ways to prepare mushrooms to release their health-protecting chemistry in Jim Meuninck's *Basic Illustrated Edible and Medicinal Mushrooms*.

Artist's Conk
Chicken of the Woods
Turkey Tail
Resinous Polypore
Reishi
Agarikon
Cauliflower Fungus

Artist's conk, Hoh Rain Forest

ARTIST'S CONK—INEDIBLE/MEDICINAL
Ganodermataceae (*Ganoderma applanatum* [Pers.] Pat.)

Origin: *Gano* is Latin for "shiny," *derma* is Greek for "skin," thus "shiny skin."

Season: Year-round; growth period in summer and fall

Identification: The artist's conk, a wood decay (saprophytic) fungus and a live sapwood pathogen (parasitic), gets its name from its white art-board-like underside. It is a woody, hard shelf mushroom, more or less flattened, with a gray to dark gray or brown top—most often brownish in the spore-producing season—the covering powder is brown spores. This shelf mushroom expands in concentric bands with a white undersurface. Old specimens can grow to 35" in circumference and 1"–8" thick.

Spores: Spores are elliptical, blunt, spore print brown; a single large artist's conk can produce 4 trillion spores annually.

Habitat: The artist's conk is an abundant brown rot mushroom in Washington growing on coniferous and deciduous trees that are standing or fallen—dead or dying trees and stumps. The mushroom attacks and decays wood, forming large shelves of fruiting bodies. Find it on western hemlock, Douglas fir, and spruce. It grows in every temperate and many subtropical forest ecosystems from North America to Africa and Asia.

Look-alikes: *Fomitopsis pinicola* bands of this species are more often orange or reddish orange, with an outer white band edge (white lipped). But this species can be grayish and dark like the artist's conk.

Inedible: Not edible, medicinal; used in traditional medicine in decoction and infusion. Aqueous extracts have antioxidant, immune-modulating, tumor-reducing chemistry. Research is ongoing.

Storage: Keep dry in sealed container.

Comments: Native Americans used the mushroom in spiritual cleansing rituals. In traditional Chinese medicine, conk extracts are used to treat lung and respiratory problems and taken as an immune-system modulator and diuretic. Artist's conk extracts are antimicrobial against *E. coli* and *Staphylococcus aureus*. It is antitumor in vitro. Decoctions are still used in several countries to treat lung and respiratory problems. Extracts have liver antitumor properties (Jeong, 2008). Artists, skilled and otherwise, use these shelf mushrooms as an expressive canvas. The white belly of the conk turns brown as it is etched by a stylus, stick, or fingernail. When burned at a campsite, it repels several varieties of insects, but I find blood root juice better for mosquitoes (Meuninck, 2013). A large artist's conk may release 30 billion brown spores per day, coloring the topside of the mushroom tan.

Recipe: Medicinal tinctures and decoctions may be made from artist's conk. Cut away the outer (present-year) growth band from the mushroom. Chop into small pieces, then try a small amount (tablespoon) in a decoction of 6 ounces of water, and simmer for 10 minutes. Or chip conk finely, place bits in a coffee filter, and pour alcohol (5 tablespoons of conk with 25% alcohol, 4-ounce pour-through) over the filtered mushroom. Capture this percolation with 5 or 6 pour-throughs. This is a mild percolation of artist's conk. Taste a small amount of the percolation or, if preferred, the decoction to see how you like it and if it likes you (for more on producing natural extractions see Jim Meuninck's *Medicinal Plants of North America* (FalconGuides, 2016).

Conk notepaper

L. conifericola in old growth

CHICKEN OF THE WOODS
Polyporaceae *(Laetiporus gilbertsonii, L. conifericola, L. sulphureus* bull. ex fr.)

Origin: *Polyporus* is Latin for "many pores." Laeti is Latin for "happy, joyful," thus "joyful pores."
Season: Late summer and fall months into Dec in Washington
Identification: There are at least 12 species of *Laetiporus*. In general, their flesh is soft when young, especially the margins, no stem, shelflike and fan shaped; color is lemon yellow to orangish. *Laetiporus gilbertsonii, L. conifericola, L. sulphureus* are parasites and/or saprophytes (brown rot) on different substrates. These 3 species have lemon- to orange-yellow top surfaces, lighter underneath. Rarely found singly but more often grouped in overlapping stemless caps. They grow to 20" or more wide on trees (I have seen one cover intermittently a 20-foot log). Shape is typically semicircular, a thick fanlike shape with margins softly rounded and undulating. Surface is radially furrowed and smooth or feltlike to the touch. Pored tubes shelter and hold spores, hence the name polypore. Pores typically yellow, and when fresh a slight squeeze will exude yellow juice. Smell is pungent, mushroomy. Mushroom color darkens with age and then fades and crumbles to white and black waste.
Spores: Spores are ovoid to elliptical, cream, white, or yellow in color.

Habitat: *L. conifericola* is found in the western Rockies to Washington. *L. sulphureus* is found east of the Rockies. *L. conifericola* is separated from the other species by its preference for conifers, especially larch (Pinaceae). *L gilbertsonii* is coastal and found in conjunction with hardwoods (eucalyptus), and *L. sulphureus* on beech and oak.

Look-alikes: All 3 species look similar, and there are at least 9 more varieties not covered here.

Edible: Choice and versatile. A meaty mushroom with a fleeting lemon flavor (slightly sour). It is best when young and tender; older mushrooms are more sour. It's a chewy, juicy mushroom that requires cleaning. If extremely dirty, pull apart segments (layers) and brush. Blanching removes any bitter taste. Texture and flavor when cooked is like chicken. Slice thin, sauté in olive oil, and eat as an entree or add to stews, soups, pizzas, and omelets. Ideal for vegetarians; goes well in risotto, curry, and various homemade salsas.

Caution: A few people have become ill eating *Laetiporus gilbertsonii*, exhibiting nausea and vomiting. Likewise, the western larch–loving variety *Laetiporus conifericola* may cause similar symptoms and tends to be a bit sour tasting. Always cook these mushrooms (see Cornell, 2006).

RECIPE

Faux Chicken

Ingredients (serves 2–3)
2 cups chicken of the woods, wiped clean with a damp cloth, then chopped
1 tbsp olive oil
3 cloves garlic, minced
2 cups tomato sauce
½ cup dry white wine
½ tsp balsamic vinegar
1 tsp soy sauce
Salt and pepper to taste

Sauté diced garlic in olive oil over medium heat, cook for 1 minute, then add mushrooms and cook for 8 to 10 minutes on medium heat, stirring occasionally. Pour in the white wine, soy, and balsamic, add the tomato sauce, and cook for another 5 minutes.

This dish may be used as a stand-alone appetizer or a sauce. If used as a spaghetti sauce, during the last 5 minutes of cooking add ¼ teaspoon fennel seed, ¼ teaspoon dried oregano, and 2 tablespoons chopped fresh basil.

See more at www.mushroom-appreciation.com/chicken-of-the-woods.html#sthash .6QhRJIGs.dpuf

Coastal dweller *L. gilbertsonii*

Medicinal: These mushrooms are antioxidant and antimicrobial; phenols inherent are anti-oxidants. They have potential as a natural antioxidant. The crude extract exhibited high anti-candida activity against *Candida albicans*, opening the possibility as a suitable antimicrobial and antioxidant agent in the food industry (Turkoglu, 2007). *L. sulphureus* showed activity against human T4 leukemic cancer cells and activity against *Plasmodium falciparum* (malaria microorganism), demonstrating possible antitumor and antimalarial activity (Lovy, 2000). Water extracts showed cancer-inhibiting activity in white mice. Mycelium is strongly antimicrobial.

Storage: Best eaten fresh. Slice thin and dry. Or sauté to remove moisture, then freeze—double-bag to prevent dehydration and freezer burn.

Comments: These mushrooms are easily spotted and found along mountain trails and in forests along beaches.

Turkey tail

TURKEY TAIL, YUN ZHI—INEDIBLE, MEDICINAL DECOCTION
Polyporaceae (*Trametes versicolor* [L.: Fries] Pilat.)

Origin: Latin *versicolor* means "changing colors" or "many colors." *Trametes* is Latin for "measuring."

Season: Year-round. Most common and collectible in Washington throughout summer and fall.

Identification: *Trametes versicolor*, also known as *Coriolus versicolor* and *Polyporus versicolor*, is a polypore, brown rot saprobe, commonly called turkey tail. The mushroom forms colonies on wood often with the caps in tiled layers. Caps are variegated, fan shaped, leathery, often fused together, with smooth to wavy margins, and exhibit a variety of colors. The mushroom when viewed from above often looks like a fanned turkey tail (hence the name) and displays concentric rows or zones of different hues; typical colors are brown, rust brown, black, blue gray, and, in older specimens, there may be green algae growth atop caps. Cap has zones of fuzzy hair. Flesh of cap is typically less than 0.13"–0.25" thick and 2"–3.5" wide. Pores are whitish to light brown, twisted, small, and numerous, 2–5 pores/millimeter.

Spore: Spore print is white.

Habitat: A common polypore mushroom found in forests throughout the world growing on stumps, dead branches, and dead trees, primarily hardwoods but occasionally on conifers—available year-round.

Look-alikes: *T. hirsute* is gray to grayish white and hairy. *T. trametes* caps are velvety to the touch. The concentric rings of *T. trametes* are different colors: white, but also brown, red, yellow, buff. *T. ochracea* lacks distinctive rings or zones of color and is reddish brown in color, or white to buff and stiffer to the touch.

Edibility: Not edible but available for medicinal preparations

Medicinal: Prepared as a medicinal tea. Sold over the counter as a medicinal supplement. Used by Chinese medical doctors to treat infection and/or inflammation of the upper respiratory tract, urinary tract, and digestive tract, and also used as therapy for chronic hepatitis and to treat general weakness of the immune system. Krestin, a proprietary anti-cancer drug approved in Japan, is extracted from the turkey tail mushroom. The US Food and Drug Administration (FDA) approved a clinical trial of turkey tail extract for patients with advanced prostate cancer to take in combination with conventional chemotherapy. Another trial pending FDA approval will test the effects of taking the extract along with a vaccine treatment in women with breast cancer (Bastyr University, 2012). The University of Texas MD Anderson Cancer Center reported that *T. versicolor* is a "promising candidate for chemoprevention due to the multiple effects on the malignant process, limited side effects and safety."

Storage: Dry and freeze or store in sealed jars.

Comments: One of the easiest mushrooms to identify and find; an attractive addition to landscaping as the fungus endures for months, even years.

Recipe: Prepare turkey tail as a decoction if chopped, or a hot infusion if powdered, or an alcohol tincture (chopped or powdered).

Resinous polypore, rubbery feel, bland taste

RESINOUS POLYPORE
Hapalopilaceae (*Ischnoderma resinosum* (Schrad.) P. Karst; *I. benzoinum*)

Origin: Latin *resinosum* meaning "resinous." *Ischnoderma* means "thin skinned," thus "thin skinned and resinous."

Season: In Washington late summer through the fall and early winter

Identification: *Ischnoderma resinosum*'s pore surface is white, and the top is brownish orange to dark brown, becoming black with age. The caps are up to 10" wide and 1" thick, often smaller. When young it is soft, thick, light colored at the edges, and shaded darker near the substrate, where it is attached without a stipe. When young and fresh this mushroom secretes brownish-amber-colored resinous water droplets. The pore surface bruises brown when young. And it is the young mushroom, fleshy and soft, that is edible. With age the mushroom becomes hard, dark, shiny, crusty, leathery, and inedible.

Spore: Spore print is white.

Habitat: *Ischnoderma resinosum* occurs on fallen and dead, sometimes long-dead, hardwood and conifer tree trunks and branches, dispersed on the dead tree singly or in overlapping clusters. It causes a white-to-yellow rot of the trees and may have an anise-like smell. Found in the fall, it is widespread in North America. *I. benzoinum* is found on conifers best in Sept–Oct.

Look-alikes: Because of its hydrated softness, the resinous polypore mushroom is unique but might be confused with reishi, lacking, however, the color of reishi or *G. tsugae*. *I. benzoinum* is similar but found specifically on conifers. Its flesh is thinner.

Edible: Flesh of young specimens is soft and juicy, rubbery touch, somewhat bland with fleeting bitterness.

Medicinal: *Ischnoderma resinosum* lectins are proteins that can be used as diagnostic probes and are highly specific to sugar and are used in wound healing and reducing scars. They are carbohydrate-binding molecules used as markers or probes in agriculture and medical research and were isolated from *Ischnoderma* in 1995. Lectins are ubiquitous in nature, holding great potential in medicine. Antibacterial and cancer inhibiting, inhibits sarcoma 180, a transplantable, nonmetastasizing tumor that is often implanted in mice for cancer research. *Ischnoderma* mushroom shows moderate inhibition of *Staphylococcus aureus* and immune-modulating health benefits (Shodhganga, 2011 pdf)

Storage: Do not store. Eat immediately.

Comments: Abundant in old-growth forests with maple and conifers—decomposing dead conifers felled by other fungi—a stellar recycler and passable survival food.

Recipe: It is best to stew this mushroom in its own juices, reducing the juice, then make gravy with the chopped mushroom and its reduced juice for venison and other wild game (add crushed juniper berries), or cook by itself with root vegetables, reducing the stew to a thick consistency. Try 2 cups of sliced mushroom, with 1 tablespoon soy, 2 tablespoons oil, 2 tablespoons white wine, 1 tablespoon dry sherry, and add one chopped garlic and one chopped shallot. Cook over low heat, first bringing out the moisture in the mushrooms, garlic, and shallot, and then reducing the broth to creamy thick richness. This should please your most discriminating guests.

Ganoderma tsugae

NORTHWEST REISHI, AMERICAN LING CHI—INEDIBLE/ MEDICINAL (WASHINGTON SPECIES)
Ganodermataceae (*Ganoderma oregonense* [Murrill]; *Ganoderma tsugae* [Murrill])

Origin: *Ganoderma* is Latin for "shiny skin." Latin *lucida* means "bright, shiny." *Tsugae* or *tsuga* is new Latin from Japanese meaning "larch."

Season: Year-round; find fresh, young mushrooms in May–Aug in Washington

Identification: These two polypores and related Asian varieties of these mushrooms, called reishi or ling chi are saprophytic brown rot fungi that break down wood by feeding on it. *G. tsugae* and *G. oregonense* may be the same species and both are kidney- or fan-shaped with a shiny red-lacquer-like sheen on the upper skin. Typically associated with either hemlocks or larch and a few other conifers, these two *Ganodermas* frequently grow at the base and on fallen logs or stumps, especially conifers. They are 4"–8" wide and attached to the substrate with a thick, hard, dark stipe.

Habitat: *G. tsugae* and *G. oregonense* grow in hemlock forests and are available year-round but best in the summer to fall when they release spores. Both *G. tsugae* and *G. lucidum* have a worldwide reputation and distribution in both tropical and temperate zones. Distribution is widespread in old-growth forests. It is cultivated both outdoors on logs and on beds of wood chips.

Look-alikes: See *Ischnoderma resinosum* above and *Fomitipsis pinacola* (red belted conk).

Medicinal: Medicinal rieshi is added to soups with bitter consequences. It is available in standardized extracts and powders for health-supportive alternative medicine therapies. Reishi has been used in traditional Chinese medicine for 2,500 years. It is considered an immune-system modulator and used for treating viral infections such as the flu (influenza), swine flu, and avian flu. Other traditional uses include treating respiratory problems (asthma and bronchitis), as well as stomach ulcers and heart disease. Reishi is antibacterial, antiviral, anti-inflammatory, antitumor, and anticancer, and is both an immune-system modulator and therapy for the immune system. Active chemistries are polysaccharides, terpenes, and other compounds contained in the mycelia and fruiting bodies.

Storage: Dried whole or powdered, in sealed containers—keep dry.

Comments: I found *G. oregonense* near Lake Ozette, Washington. Purchase *Ganoderma* species, the whole mushroom and powders, at Asian markets and online.

Recipe: Mushrooms and recipes available online. The hard and dry mushroom is powdered and chemistry is drawn with a water decoction or with a long hot infusion, like a tea.

Ganoderma oregonense budding on an old-growth hemlock

17-inch wide *L. officinalis*

AGARIKON, QUININE CONK, LARCH BRACKET MUSHROOM, BROWN TRUNK ROT, EBURIKO—INEDIBLE, MEDICINAL

Fomitopsidaceae (*Laricifomes officinalis* [Vill. Kotyl & Pouzar] [Synonym: *Fomitopsis officinalis* Villars: FR.] Bondartsev & Singer)

Origin: Latin *fomentum* means "tinder"; *officinale* means "medicinal uses."

Season: Available year-round, actively spore producing in late summer and fall

Identification: *Laricifomes officinalis* is a large bracket fungus found on the trunks of coniferous hosts, where it causes a brown rot. Fruiting bodies persist and become larger and larger, building layer upon layer over time—specimens may be 16" x 18" (see photo) and a few up to 20" long and nearly as wide. Sporophores (the mushroom's spore-producing body) are large. These distinctive conks are columnar or hoof shaped. They are soft, yellow-white when young, but soon becoming white and chalky. The decay produced by the fungus is brown, cubically cracked, with thick white felt like material in large cracks. Taste of the mushroom itself is very bitter.

Spore: The spore color is white.

Habitat: Available year-round, found in old growths on conifers in the northwestern United States, and is perhaps extinct in most of Asia and Europe. It is becoming rare within the old-growth forests of Washington, Oregon, Montana, Idaho, and British Columbia due to harvesting of old-growth trees.

Look-alikes: Younger specimens similar to *Fomitopsis pinicola*

Inedible: Not edible except as a tea or medicinal extract

Medicinal: Shows notable low minimum inhibitory concentrations against *Mycobacterium tuberculosis* complex (Hwang, 2013). Agaricin from the mushroom is an anhidrotic, anti-inflammatory, and a parasympatholytic nerve agent. Pharmaceutical companies produce agaricin synthetically. Alcohol tinctures of the powdered mushroom appear effective as a smooth muscle relaxant for stomach cramps. Homeopathic doses may be effective against night sweats, pancreatic inflammation, and liver inflammation cramps (Rogers, 2011).

Storage: Dried and powdered in sealed containers or gelatin capsules

Comments: Shame on me! I picked the agarikon (first photo) from a larch and have lived to regret it. They are rare and so are old growths. I tried to compensate by collecting spores from the specimen and spreading them around the bases and wounds in larch trees. Did any of the spores fruit? I don't know. But about 30 larches were inoculated in Washington, Idaho, and Montana (near Glacier National Park). Agarikon is now being produced in laboratory cultures. Native Americans referred to the fungi as "bread of ghosts" or "tree biscuits." Spiritual references to the special powers of the mushroom and its hanging fruiting bodies are documented. Shamans and spiritual leaders hung hand-carved fruiting bodies, representing spiritual figures, and spirit catchers with large open mouths and stomachs from dance lodge walls and ceilings to capture spirits and protect the people. Upon the shaman's death, the people buried the mushroom with the shaman.

Recipe: Seek medicinal preparation online, ready to use

L. officinalis on an old-growth larch

Cauliflower fungus attacking Douglas fir HUGH SMITH

CAULIFLOWER FUNGUS
Sparrassidaceae (*Sparassis radicata*, Weir)

Origin: From Greek word *sparassein* meaning to tear. *Radicata* means rooting.

Season: Summer, fall

Identification: A parasitic fungus in the order Polyporales that attacks Douglas fir and pine roots (brown cubical rot). It emerges from a rootlike base and spreads (expands). Specimens have been found weighing more than 50 pounds. Its unique shape helps identify the species. Many foragers (as the name implies) call it cauliflower fungus. Trudell and Ammirati, in their excellent field guide *Mushrooms of the Pacific Northwest*, describe the numerous wavy branches as egg noodle–like. They have obviously eaten cauliflower and know the difference. I concur with *their* description. Individual flat, wavy branches are pale and creamy colored. Fruiting body is a mass of wavy and curled lobes giving the overall effect of cauliflower, cabbage, or egg noodles. Once you find it you will have little trouble identifying the species. A difficult find, however.

Spores: Smooth, oval, and white

Habitat: In conifer forests and associated with and attacking Douglas fir and pines

Look-alikes: Its unique shape helps it stand alone and makes it easy to identify. There are two eastern relatives, *Sparassis herbstii* and *Sparassis crispa*.

Edible: For me, a rare but delightful find, pleasing to the palate. Be certain the specimen is young and tender.

Storage: Dry in an air dryer. Best eaten fresh.

Comments: Begin your search around Douglas firs. It attacks roots.

RECIPE

Cauliflower Tempura

Cooking oil
Tempura batter
Cauliflower fungus
Soy sauce
Yellow mustard

Purchase a package of tempura coating. Cut the cauliflower fungus into chunks, then coat as per the directions on the package and deep-fry. Use soy sauce and yellow mustard (blend the 2 ingredients) as a condiment.

2   Chanterelles

Ridges of a chanterelle

Chanterelles are small to large mushrooms with primitive spore-producing folds instead of gills. The folds or ridges of chanterelles, unlike the gills on gilled mushrooms, are integrated with and part of the stem and cap. In addition, chanterelle ridges may be attached irregularly to the stem, starting where they please, a few lower on the stem, others higher up. This irregular pattern of chanterelle ridges is distinct from the regular attachment of gills to the caps in gilled mushrooms. These integrated ridges, unlike gills, are not easily torn, pulled off, or removed from the stipe (stem) or cap—they are integrated and part of it.

Pacific Golden Chanterelle
Black Trumpet
Winter Chanterelle
White Chanterelle
Pig's Ear
Wholly Chanterelle

Golden chanterelle found in Mount Baker Wilderness

PACIFIC GOLDEN CHANTERELLE
Cantharellaceae (*Cantharellus formosus* C.)

Origin: Latin *formosus*, meaning "beautiful, handsome, well formed"
Season: Late summer, fall, winter
Identification: *C. formosus*, cap 1"–6" wide and larger to 3" tall, at first convex then flattened with depressed center (broadly convex to vase shaped). Margin is inrolled and wavy. Color varies from yellow to pale orange yellow, cinnabar red, or peach. Surface is dry and smooth or tomentose (covered with minute matted filaments). No true gills, but false wrinkled, veined, and cross-veined ridges descending the stem; that is, the wrinkles or folds in the mushroom's surface are not separate and distinct from the cap and stem. Stem is without ring and near in color to the cap and tapers on its way down. Underside of cap is orange to pale yellow. Cap bruises brownish. Odor hints of fruit—perhaps apricot, but odor may be absent. Flesh is firm and solid, white to pale yellow, with no change in color when sliced. Taste is mild to peppery. Faintly fruity odor. Widely available in markets, an easy place to get a first look.
Spores: Ellipsoid spores leave a white to pale yellow spore print.
Habitat: Found growing throughout North America on the ground in coniferous and deciduous forests as mycorrhizal partners with oak and fir trees, from late June to Aug in the eastern United States, Sept–Nov in Washington, and Nov–Feb in California. They grow singly, scattered, or in colonies.

Look-alikes: The gilled mushroom *Hygrophoropsis aurantiaca* (false chanterelle) is similar to *C. formosus* and toxic (see p. 97, Ammirati, 2009). *Chroogomphus tomentosus* is not desirable: soft, bland, with little taste.

Edibility: Tastes floral, smells fruity, and is abundant. Prepare without washing—brush clean—and stir-fry, or sauté in butter and/or olive oil. Then dip into or drizzle with warm Brie cheese. Chanterelles complement meat, poultry, fish, and shellfish.

Medicinal: Chanterelles are relatively high in potassium and vitamin C and rich in vitamin D2. Their potassium content makes them a good addition to a blood-pressure-lowering diet. The alcoholic (methanol and ethanol) extracts of *Cantharellus cibarius* (and *C. formosus*) have antioxidant, antimicrobial, and other phytochemical potentials. Extracts contain phenols, terpenoids, flavonoids, alkaloids, anthraquinones, and saponins. Both methyl and ethanol extracts inhibited *Escherichia coli* and *Candida albicans* in vitro—and the methanol extract also inhibited the growth of *Salmonella typhi*, indicating a broader spectrum of activity from the methanol extract. The ethanol extract possessed greater antifungal activity, however. *C. cibarius* also possesses bioactive metabolites and phytochemical antioxidants capable of scavenging free radicals (Aina et al., 2012). Research suggests that chanterelles have insecticidal properties but are harmless to humans.

Storage: Best fresh but holds up to refrigeration and drying. An hour's exposure to sunlight may increase the vitamin D2 content, improving its nutritional value.

Chanterelles at Pike Place Market, photo taken in August 2014

Comments: In the early 18th century, chanterelles entered the palace kitchens of Versailles. Leftovers were placed at the gate and given to peasants. In time the food gifts imparted the French population with their rich taste for fine cuisine. In Bhutan chanterelles are cooked with cheese and chili peppers.

RECIPE

Golden Chanterelle Sandwich

Golden chanterelles
Butter
White wine
1 slice bacon
Pinch of thyme
Clove of garlic, minced
Two slices bread, toasted

Sauté golden chanterelles in butter and white wine with a slice of bacon. Remove mushrooms and bacon and reduce cooking juices to a sauce. Gently warm the mushrooms in the reduction. Toss mushrooms with a pinch of thyme and a minced garlic clove. Spread mushrooms on toast; garnish with aioli or mayonnaise, sliced tomato, and sautéed onions.

Golden Chanterelle Sandwich

Black trumpet, "aerial truffle"

BLACK TRUMPET
Cantharellaceae (*Craterellus species O1*; *Craterellus fallax* formerly *C. cornucopioides*)

Origin: *Craterellus* is Greek for "cup, drinking vessel"; *cornucopioides* refers to "cornucopia" or horn of plenty; *fallax* means "deceptive."

Season: Fall, winter

Identification: Thin-fleshed, fragrant, and funnel-shaped mushrooms—small to medium size, up to 4" tall and 3" wide. Flesh is leathery and becomes somewhat brittle with age, parchment-like. Lower end of the stem is pinched. Cap and stem integrated and not separately defined. They grow singly but more often in tight clusters or groups of clusters (keep looking, there are more). *C. species O1* is a West Coast species. It first appears tubelike and then takes on a deep vase appearance, with upper edge rolled under. Flesh is smoky brown to black or dark gray. Surface is smooth or scaly with fibers or dark scales over a grayish to gray-brown base. Outer surface is smooth to slightly wrinkled when older. Funnel may open and become wavy at maturity.

Spores: Variable: print is salmon colored, yellowish, white, or cream colored

Habitat: Washington is a tough place to find black trumpets (*Craterellus species O1*). They may be found along the southern coast in association with madrone, tan oaks, and mature conifers surrounded by luxurious moss. They may also have a symbiotic (mycorrhizal) relationship with these trees and moss. Southern Oregon is better and Northern California is good.

East of the Rockies, old-growth beech forest with sphagnum moss is best. Look in southern coastal areas and you may get lucky. This saprobe grows from the ground, typically up through moss, and perhaps having a symbiotic relationship with it and the host tree.

Look-alikes: Can be confused with blue chanterelle, *Polyozellus multiplex*, which is also edible. East of the Rockies, Devil's urn, *Urnula craterium*, is toxic and appears in the spring.

Edible: The flavor of black truffles is excellent when dried and crushed as a condiment over savory dishes. Excellent crumbled on pizza. Crush fine, sauté in butter, and press into soft cheese. Allow to infuse for 24 hours in the refrigerator, then serve. For your first effort, sauté and get a taste of the flavor—new ideas will emerge. In French cuisine they are prepared in terrine (like meat loaf). Also used in marinades, dressings, and as an integral ingredient in Moroccan tagine dishes and fricassees.

Storage: Very good dried, increasing its shelf life—can be frozen too.

Comments: The mushroom's nutrient profile (per 100 g): 13.4 g carbohydrates including mannitol and sugar, 4.9 g fat, 69.5 g protein, with 378 calories and 87 mg of vitamin C. Health-promoting nutrients include polyunsaturated fats and phenolic compounds, including numerous flavonoids. One undocumented source reported the mushroom stimulates the body to metabolize stored fat. Although difficult to find, these mushrooms show up at the same sites every fall. Once you discover them, you have an annual source. They grow on moss and in pine duff and show up better than most field guides suggest. Look for moss forming a north-side mantle around conifers and oaks and in the eastern United States, around the base of large beech trees.

Eastern black trumpet on its substrate moss

RECIPE

Mushroom Chiles Rellenos

Cooking oil
4 poblano peppers, roasted
1 cup dried black trumpet mushrooms
Salt and pepper
½ medium sweet onion, chopped
1 cup mozzarella cheese
½ cup Swiss cheese, chopped
¼ cup mild salsa
1 tsp soy sauce
2 tbsp Cholula or other hot sauce

Remove skin and seeds from roasted peppers. Sauté mushrooms and onion. Mix cheeses, soy sauce, salsa, hot sauce, cooked mushrooms, and onion. Preheat oven to 450°F. Place stuffed peppers in a pan; bake in oven for 8–10 minutes, depending on size of peppers.

Poblanos stuffed with black trumpets or other mushrooms

Put on your coat and hat and go search for this winter beauty. HUGH SMITH

WINTER CHANTERELLE, YELLOWFOOT
Cantharellaceae (*Craterellus tubaeformis* [Fries] Quel.)

Origin: From Latin *tuba*, meaning "tube" or "trumpet shaped"

Season: Late summer, fall, winter in southern range Washington

Identification: Small trumpet-shaped (funnel) mushroom, brown to yellowish or orangish brown, growing in groups and scattered. Flesh is thin. It is mycorrhizal with conifers. Spore-producing folds (false gills) are decurrent and branched, running down stem and attached to it. Stem 1½"–3" long and 1½"–2¾" wide. False gills are grayish. Margin of cap inrolled, center depressed. Stipe (stem) is yellow and hollow, distinctive.

Spores: Spore print is white.

Look-alikes: Similar to *C. infundibuliformis* with its lemon-yellow and hollow stipe and slightly darker spore print (buff), which is also considered edible.

Habitat: Found in cool, wet montane areas and lowland coniferous bogs, residing on decayed logs and piercing through moss above decaying logs. Look in western hemlock and Douglas fir stands in thick mats of decaying wood.

Edible: Small but choice, they grow in groups and you will need plenty to feed the crowd. Complements meat dishes and is an excellent addition to soups and hearty stews. Great with oil or white pasta sauces over your choice of pasta. Try the mushrooms sautéed and place on half a bagel laced with smoked-salmon cream cheese. Top with a thin slice of tomato and throw a few capers over the mushrooms with thin slices of red onion.

Comments: Washington is blessed with access to many chanterelles. They are fairly easy to identify and exciting to find.

RECIPE

Simple Salmon

¾ pound king salmon fillet
2 cups winter chanterelles, halved lengthwise
4 tbsp butter
1 tbsp soy sauce
1 tsp fresh ginger, minced
1 minced shallot
3 tbsp sherry
3 tbsp of olive oil
2–3 oz. water

Season salmon lightly with salt, then brown both sides in butter. Set rare piece of fish aside. In same pan, blend soy, ginger, and sherry. Roll mushrooms in the combination, soaking them. Leave them in the pan, and then add olive oil, shallot, and garlic. Sauté the mushrooms at medium to low heat for about 6–7 minutes, adding enough water to keep everything wet. Push mushrooms to the side and return salmon to pan to reheat. Serve salmon with mushroom sauce.

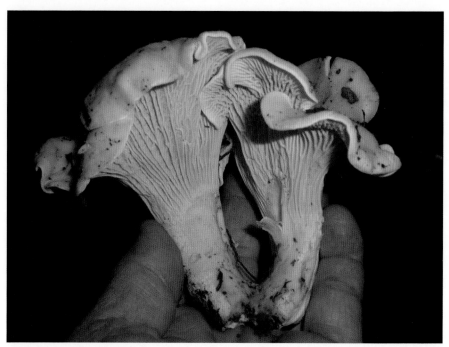
White chanterelle HUGH SMITH

WHITE CHANTERELLE
Cantharellaceae (*Cantharellus subalbidus* AH Sm. and Morris)

Origin: *Subalbidus* means "whitish."

Season: Fall, early winter

Identification: Cream- to white-colored cap and stipe, changing to yellow orange when dry and/or old. Flesh bruises yellow to orange. Shape typical of chanterelles (vase shaped), medium-size cap 2"–5" wide, to 5" tall, stipe ¾"–2", cap flat to depressed with wavy margin. Spores borne on distinct decurrent folds or ridges (not true gills). Yellow older specimens can be confused with *C. formosus*. Taste is mild, slightly fruity.

Spores: Elliptical-shaped, white spores

Habitat: Mycorrhizal with conifers in old growth, especially at low elevation in Washington coastal areas. Partners with hemlock, madrone, and specifically Douglas fir; found singly, scattered, or grouped in coniferous duff.

Look-alikes: Looks similar to *C. cascadensis* and *C. formosus*. Similar species include clitocybes and hygrophorus, which, however, have true gills.

Edible: Choice edible, one of the best. Cut into sizable chunks and bake at 350°F for 10 minutes. Cook with pork, chicken, eggs, lamb, beef, or veal. Vegetarians sauté with Chinese cabbages including bok choy.

Storage: Dry in food dryer, reconstitute in water, and cook in the same water. Alternative: Bake or sauté, then freeze. When ready to prepare, throw frozen mushrooms right into the pan—do not thaw as this softens the texture. Keep fresh mushrooms in a paper sack when refrigerated.

Comments: A prized find. Studies show that old-growth conifers, 300 or more years old, are more likely to harbor larger numbers of *C. subalbidus* than second growth or new growth.

RECIPE

Versaille Sauté of Chanterelles

½ pound white chanterelles
¼ cup duck or goose fat (bacon fat will work)
2 tbsp dry sherry
1 large chopped shallot

Clean mushrooms with a brush, pick free of insects and larvae, slice thin, and sauté slowly in goose or duck fat with the chopped shallot and dry sherry. Turn frequently until the mushrooms absorb the oil and wine, then remove mushrooms, simmer juices to a thick reduction, and spread over mushrooms.

Pig's ear in pine duff. Find in the Mount Adams area. HUGH SMITH

PIG'S EAR
Cantharellaceae *(Gomphus clavatus* [Fr.] SFG)

Origin: *Gomphus* means "hinged" and *clavatus* means "striped."

Season: Fall

Identification: Typically, two or more tan caps, irregularly shaped, rising from the same stipe, edges fused, caps tan with distinctive purplish veins or folds (false gills, or ridges) beneath; the undersurface is wrinkled, purplish to lilac, fading with age to lilac. Mushroom is somewhat vase shaped with crowded and irregular veins (ridges), margin wavy. It grows to 7" tall and is up to 6" wide. Lower part of stem is whitish and changing toward lilac near the upper portion of the cap's undersurface. Bottom and sides densely covered with purple-colored folds (veins) that produce spores.

Spores: Spores print ochre

Look-alikes: Distinctive in its range

Habitat: Found in gregarious groups in coniferous moist areas and mycorrhizal with spruce and fir. Begin your search in wet, shady areas with deep decaying humus at moderate altitudes plus or minus 2000'—available across the entire northern montane region of America.

Edible: Choice edible. Pictured species was infected with insects, which is typical. Find them early as older groups are consumed by larvae and insects. Don't let that bother you, however; brush clean, slice, and stir fry with shallots—also an excellent pickling mushroom.

Medicinal: This is an antifungal mushroom worth eating that in trials inhibits sarcoma 180 and Ehrlich carcinoma in vivo (Rogers, 2011, p. 189).

Storage: Dry, seal, and freeze. Store in a paper bag and eat within 3 days when fresh.

Comments: When I cross coniferous wetlands en route to secret fly-fishing streams, pig's ears are the bonus.

RECIPE

Pickled Pig's Ears

(Pickling Recipe—makes 3 quarts)
3–4 pounds pig's ears
3 cups white vinegar, 5% acidity
2 cups water
3½ tbsp canning and pickling salt
3 tsp black peppercorns
1 chopped onion
3 garlic cloves

Cut and discard mushroom ends, rinse mushrooms in cold water, and drain. In Pyrex or stainless-steel pot, combine water, salt, and vinegar—heat and stir to dissolve salt, then add mushrooms and chopped onion. Bring to a boil and simmer for 10 minutes. Pluck out a mushroom and check for tenderness. If it is too tough, simmer for another 2 minutes. In each sterilized quart jar, add 1 tablespoon peppercorns and 1 garlic clove. Place mushrooms in jars to about ¾ inch from the lip and then cover with pickling juice. Remove air bubbles with a nonferrous knife or spatula. Wipe jar mouth and lids clean, adjust tightness, and process for 20 minutes; add 10 minutes of processing for altitudes over 1,000 feet.

T. floccosus

WHOLLY CHANTERELLE
Cantharellaceae (*Turbinellus floccosus* [Schweinitz] Singer and *Turbinellus kauffmanii* (Smith) Peterson)

Origin: *Turbinellus* means "spinning top." *Floccosus* is Latin for "flock of wool" or Greek for "plug." *Kauffmanii* is German for "merchant."
Season: Summer, fall
Identification: These 2 species are separated from *Gomphus* and are closely related or even of the same genus. *T. kauffmanii* is a tall chanterelle-like mushroom from 2" to 6" wide at the top of the fruit and up to 8" tall. Its inner cup is lined with numerous coarse scales, and it does not grow in clusters. A robust species that is somewhat rare. *T. floccosus* is more common, shorter, more delicate, with fewer, less coarse scales, and grows alone or in clusters. Both are trumpet shaped. Hollow interior of the "trumpet" is covered with wool or cotton-like scales (see photos). Top slightly depressed when young and hollow when mature. Ventral side is deep ridged. Color inside red to orange (reddish orange and fading with age) and outside fertile surface is whitish to cream to yellowish colored. Wholly scales are distinctive, larger, and coarser in *T. kauffmanii*. *T. floccosus* is gregarious and found in clusters and occasionally in fairy rings. The difference of size of the scales of the wholly interiors of the cups are indicative. Even so, separating the species in different growth stages may be difficult.
Spores: Ochre

Habitat: Conifer forest, often in association with hemlock. Grows on the ground and not trees.

Look-alikes: Looks like a golden chanterelle but differentiated by wholly scales

Edible: Edibility of *T. kauffmanii* is questionable, sour tasting, and said to cause stomach upset, diarrhea, and nausea in many cases. Hmmm. Enough said. *Turbinellus floccosus* is said to be little better, however, and this is a favorite mushroom of Mexicans, Indians (India), and Nepalese Sherpas.

Medicinal: It is sold in markets and on the streets in these countries. The Mexican species lives in association to *Abies religiosa*, and this unique pairing may be the reason why eating *T. floccosus* does not adversely affect Mexicans. Other sources say people having consumed this mushroom for hundreds of years (if not thousands of years) are immune to its toxic chemistry. Given all this I cannot recommend this mushroom as food.

Storage: Dry, seal, and freeze. Store fresh in paper bag.

Caution: Contains an insoluble, undigestible, nor-caperoic acid that enlarge tumors in mice.

Comments: This species varies in color and density of scales. Color fades as it ages. It is abundant on Heliotrope Trail in Mount Baker Wilderness. It appears to show even In dry spells.

Recipe: Not recommended as food

Cutaway of *T. kauffmanii*

3   Tooth Fungi

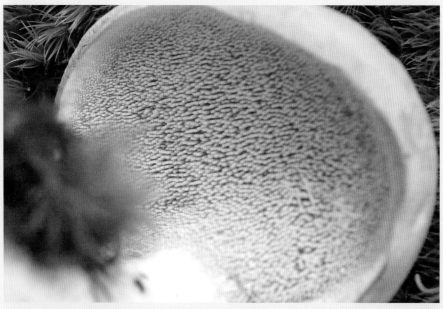

Teeth of *Hydnum* tooth fungus

This group of mushrooms bears spores on teeth-like projections called spines or pendants. They are in the phylum Basidiomycota and produce spores in basidiocarps. Covered here are the almost unmistakable edible species: *Hericium erinaceus* and *Hydnum repandum*—the hedgehog mushroom—which is more closely related to chanterelles.

Conifer Bear's Head
Lion's Mane Tooth Fungi
Hedgehog
Belly Button Hedgehog
Floccosus

Hericium coralloides is rare and spectacular.

CONIFER BEAR'S HEAD
Hericiaceae (*Hericium abietis* [Weir ex. Hubert] K. A. Harrison)

Origin: *Hericium* means "shaggy" and abietis means "fir" as in fir tree or fir duff
Season: Late summer and fall in Washington
Identification: Large from 10" to 30" tall, creamy white to buff (specimens found to over 80 pounds, but typically smaller). A white saprophytic conifer wood decomposer, typically found on hemlock and fir. Head is branched. Spines are numerous, descending, giving the appearance of a frozen waterfall or the head of a white weeping willow. Spines become yellowish with age. Spines up to 2".
Spore: White spore, white spore print
Habitat: Conifer forests on dead trees, logs, stumps of hemlock and fir, primarily fir
Look-alikes: *H. erinaceus* (next) and *H. coralloides* are similar and all edible. *H. coralloides*, with shorter teeth (1 cm or less) is a parasitic saprophyte on hardwoods and is rarely found in Washington, a challenge (see photo).
Edible: Deliciously different. Cook slowly, low heat.
Medicinal: This mushroom is rich in physiologically active compounds, especially beta-glucan polysaccharides, which are responsible for anticancer, immunomodulating, hypo-lipidemic (antidiabetic), antioxidant, and neuroprotective activities. *H. erinaceus* (next) is also reported to have antimicrobial, antihypertensive, and wound-healing properties. *H. erinaceus* extracts show promise fighting pancreatitis and certain cancers, including intestinal, pancreatic, and esophageal cancers. When taken in the course of chemotherapy, extracts significantly reduced the side effects, such as fatigue, sickness, and nausea.

RECIPE

Toothy Tapas

If tasting for the first time, cook slowly (low heat) in bubbling butter. My favorite tooth recipe is tapas-style on sourdough bread toast points.

1 or 2 tooth fungi
1 tbsp each butter and olive oil
Thinly sliced small red potato
Mayo and Dijon
Thinly sliced sweet onion, small amount on each toast point
Arugula
Tapatio

Sauté mushroom, onion, and potato in butter and olive oil. Spread mayo on one half of toast and Dijon on the other. Arrange 3 or 4 potato slices on toast, cover with arugula and onion, and then hold it all in place with pieces of the mushroom. Put some hot sauce on the side. Salt and pepper to taste.

Toothy Tapas

Sweet, rich in umami, delicious—conifer bear's head HUGH SMITH

Comments: Finding one bear's head or a lion's mane makes my season. These are delicious mushrooms slow cooked in butter, sweet, fragrant, and satisfying. Replanting of logged firs with pines is reducing habitat.

Lion's mane, *Hericium erinaceus*

LION'S MANE TOOTH FUNGI, BEARDED TOOTH
Hericiaceae (*Hericium erinaceus* [Bulliard: Fries] Persoon)

Origin: Latin *hericium* means "hedgehog" or "shaggy"; *erinaceus* means "hedgehog."
Season: Late summer and fall in Washington
Identification: Generally, a solitary white rot saprobe, 2"–20" across, a white, toothy mushroom that yellows with age. It presents as a cascade of dangling white spines (pendulous icicle-like teeth), which give this fungus its common name. Spines may be up to 2" long, and they give the fungus the appearance of a lion's mane or a frozen waterfall. Mushroom is attached to tree with a thick, tough, and solid central stalk.
Spore: White spore, white spore print

Habitat: This mushroom is found singly and occasionally in pairs on a wound in a live deciduous tree (hardwood), primarily oak, maple, and in the East beech. Rare in Washington along the coast on oak. The species is found in the western, eastern, and southern states—available also in mushroom growth kits at Washington farmer's markets or online.

Look-alikes: *H. americanum, H coralloides* are similar and all edible.

Edible: A delicious, sweet-tasting mushroom, lion's mane is succulent, the texture pleases the palate, and the mild flavor makes it one of the best edible mushrooms. Sauté and eat by itself or serve hot in a vegetarian sandwich. Soften mushroom with cooking, which also rids some of the water from these hydrated specimens. It goes well with lemony marinades.

Medicinal: *H. erinaceus* is reported to have antimicrobial, antihypertensive, and wound-healing properties. *H. erinaceus* extracts show promise fighting pancreatitis and certain cancers, including intestinal, pancreatic, and esophageal cancers. When taken in the course of chemotherapy, extracts significantly reduced the side effects, such as fatigue, sickness, and nausea. In addition, *H. erinaceus* may counter osteoporosis. Of interest to multiple sclerosis researchers is that myelination was also enhanced. The anti-inflammatory chemistry of lion's mane may be useful to curb inflammation and cool gastric and esophageal ulcers (Yang, Newman et al., 2011).

Storage: Best eaten immediately. Store and freeze in prepared dish, double-wrap to prolong storage longevity.

Comments: Native Americans used the dried powder of the mushroom to stem bleeding (styptic); powder was carried in a leather pouch as a first-aid kit.

Recipe: This mushroom is best sautéed. It is typically clean when found and does not require cleaning. Cut away the base, which is often clogged with woody fiber. Then slice the mushroom in ¼" slices from top to bottom, lightly coat with cake flour, then sauté at medium heat until mushroom browns. Eat with a fork—simple, satisfying, and healthful. See appendix A for more ideas.

Hedgehog, a toothy delight HUGH SMITH

HEDGEHOG, WOOD HEDGEHOG, SWEET TOOTH
Hydnaceae (*Hydnum repandum* L.)

Origin: Latin *hydnei* means "those with spines or tubercles"; *repandum* means "spreading."
Season: Summer to autumn
Identification: *H. repandum* is mycorrhizal and symbiotic with hardwoods and conifers; it prefers fir trees but is also found in association with deciduous trees. It shows an orange, yellow, or tan cap up to 7" wide, typically smaller, studded underneath with teeth—a defining feature. It is easy for beginners to recognize. The *H. repandum* in the photo shows spines running down the stipe, though this is not always typical of what you will find. The spines may be absent from the stipe. It is an edible mushroom with no poisonous look-alikes, somewhat irregular in shape, concave or convex with a wavy margin that is inrolled when young. Shape of the cap becomes more irregular when crowded in clusters. Cap surface is generally dry and smooth, with mature specimens displaying cracks. Flesh is white, thick, firm, but brittle, and bruises yellow to orange brown. Spines are slender, small, whitish, measuring 0.1"–0.3" long. On close inspection spines may run down the stem on one side or all sides. Stem is 1.2"–3.9" long and 0.4"–1.2" thick, either white or the same color as the cap, and may be off-center. Spores are smooth, roughly spherical to broadly egg-shaped, and may contain a single oil droplet.
Spore: Spore print is cream white, spores smooth and spherical.

Habitat: The fruiting bodies grow singly or in groups (and occasionally in fairy rings) on the ground or in leaf litter in both deciduous and coniferous forests. They are closely related to chanterelles and found with or near them. They are widely distributed in the northern temperate areas as well as Australia, Europe, and northern Asia.

Look-alikes: There are two edible look-alikes: a pure white variety of this species, *H. repandum* var. *album*, and the giant hedgehog (*Hydnum albomagnum*). *H. albidum* has a white to pale yellowish-gray fruit body that bruises yellow to orange. *H. albomagnum* is large and paler than *H. repandum*.

Edible: Good to very good with a sweet, nutty taste and crunchy texture. Brush the cap and stipe after harvest and avoid getting soil stuck between the mushroom's teeth.

Medicinal: Chemical diepoxide shows cytotoxic activity against several tumor cell lines in vitro, including sarcoma 180 cancer cell lines and Ehrlich carcinoma (Dembitsky et. al., Elsevier GmbH, 2013). Chloroform extracts of the fungus show mild antibiotic effect against *Enterobacter aerogenes*, various staphylococcus organisms, *S. epidermidis*, and *Bacillus subtilis* (Takahashi, Endo, and Nozoe, 1992). At the molecular level, repandiol, an alkylating agent, inserts cross-links between strands of DNA, making it difficult for the genetic material to express or replicate (Millard et al., 2004). European studies conducted after the 1986 Chernobyl (Ukraine) meltdown have shown the fruit bodies have a high rate of accumulation of the radioactive isotope cesium (Stachowiak, 2012).

Storage: Eating fresh is best. Keep for 3 days in refrigerator. Cook, double-wrap, and freeze.

Comments: *Hydnum* species are more closely related genetically and taste-wise to chanterelles. In France the mushroom's common name is *pied-de-mouton* (mutton's foot). Mexico, Spain, and Canada also market the mushroom. It is a favorite with wild ungulates and squirrels. The Swiss consider the mushroom psychoactive.

Recipes: This is a versatile mushroom that tastes great alone. It also may be pickled or simmered in stocks, where it takes the flavors from the other ingredients. The fungus may be dried and ground into powder and used as a pepper substitute; use the powder to flavor roasts, steaks, soups, and chili. Freeze or dry for storage. Older caps respond to boiling or cooking in butter, which helps eliminate their bitterness. Specimens found under conifers may taste stronger. Hedgehog has a very high food value of 434 kilocalories per 100 g.

Hydnum with lateral, spineless stem

Belly button hedgehog, a tooth fungus HUGH SMITH

BELLY BUTTON HEDGEHOG
Hydnaceae (*Hydnum umbilicatum* Peck)

Origin: Latin: "spines of the bellybutton" (roughly)
Season: Summer, Sept, Oct, Nov
Identification: Small mushroom, cap 1"–2" wide, convex, spreading to broadly convex, and mycorrhizal with conifers in Washington. Cap is pale orange to cream with a central depression, belly button–like. This is a toothed fungus. Teeth are the hymenophore, the spore-producing body. Stipe is proportionally long and thinner than *H. repandum* to 2" in length and ¼"–½" wide and is stout and firm.
Spores: White spores, white spore print
Habitat: Mycorrhizal (symbiotic) with conifers and oaks, scattered in distribution
Look-alikes: See *Hydnum repandum* (above), a similar but larger tooth fungus. Both are edible.
Edible: Choice edible, sweet and peppery, but bitter if too old
Medicinal: They are antibacterial, anti-inflammatory, and increase energy, thereby combating fatigue.
Storage: Store in prepared dishes, frozen
Comments: In Washington find these mushrooms scattered with conifers. In habitats of the East, they are more frequently found as partners with oaks.

RECIPE

Belly Button Pita Pizza

3 pieces pita bread (makes 3 personal-size pizzas)
4 tbsp olive oil
16 oz. crushed tomatoes
1 garlic clove (or 2 for garlic lovers)
½ tsp fennel seeds
1 tsp each fresh basil and oregano (or ¼ tsp each of dried)
½ tsp soy sauce
1 tbsp Riesling sweet or dry
¼ tsp balsamic vinegar
2 cups mozzarella cheese
20 to 25 belly button mushrooms
¼ cup sliced green olives
½ cup Crescenzago cheese
¼ cup Parmesan cheese

For the crust, let's try something different. Pita bread. Brush the pita bread with olive oil, and then spread seasoned tomato sauce over the pita. To make the sauce for three pitas: Simmer in a pan a 16-ounce can of crushed tomatoes with 1 chopped garlic clove, ½ teaspoon of fennel seeds, and ¼ teaspoon each of dried oregano and basil (fresh is better and 4 times the amount), ½ teaspoon of soy sauce, 1 tablespoon of white wine, and ¼ teaspoon of balsamic vinegar. Whew! That's the sauce. Simmer to thicken. Spread cooled sauce on pita, place belly button slices all around, then slice green olives thinly, about 4 or 5 slices per pizza, and place slices between mushrooms. Drizzle lightly again with quality olive oil, add mozzarella, and then bake at 500°F for 10–12 minutes or until pita begins to brown. Pull pizzas and add dollops of Crescenza Italian cheese (room temperature), then blanket with fresh-grated Parmesan cheese. Serve.

Suaveolens with bluish-purple stipe found streamside under alder in the North Cascades

FLOCCOSUS
Bankeraceae (*Hydnellum suaveolens* [Scop] Karst)

Origin: *Hydnum* means "spined," and *suaveolens* means "sweet smelling, fragrant"
Season: Summer and fall
Identification: White tooth fungus with brownish teeth under cap and running down stipe. Center of cap browns as it ages. Amorphous shape. It is mycorrhizal especially with Sitka spruce (the specimen shown found near Engelmann spruce). It may grow singly or in small groups. Cap may be single or fused with others, from 3" to 8" wide. Cap sculpted with wrinkles, pits and canals, ridges and lumps. Stipe is irregular to cylindrical, purplish blue, and may turn blue black when pinched or handled—color is indicative. Taste is faintly minty. Flesh is white to brown bluish in stem. And the external two layers of cap are whitish and dull orange. Mushroom is spongy or corkish in feel and texture.
Spores: Spore print brown
Habitat: Found under spruce and other conifers and often along streams and dwelling under bushy alder. Widely distributed over western North America—typically a coastal species associated with Sitka spruce.
Look-alikes: Older species may look like *Hydnellum auranticum* and *Hydnellum aurantile*, not covered in this text.
Edible: Not edible, too tough and unpleasant tasting. No known medicinal uses.

Spines of *Hydnellum suaveolens*

Storage: Eat immediately or dry in an electric dryer and seal in glass jars.

Comments: I included this specimen because it is an excellent dye. For those interested, go to http://riihivilla.blogspot.com/2008/02/hydnellum-suaveolens-tuoksuorakasvrjyst.html. It is also of interest because edible tooth fungi are easy to identify, but there are inedible species such as *H. suaveolens* that are not. Know the difference. This pictured specimen was far from its typical home in a reclusive domain, hidden under shrubs, at high altitude where there were no Sitka spruces, on the east side of the Cascades.

4   Boletes (Boletales) Boletus; Leccinum and Suillus

Edible bolete

BOLETES are mushrooms with spore-emitting pores on the underside of the cap—not gills. When cut in cross section, the pored tubes become evident. Tubes release from the cap with a pinch and pull. Boletes are typically found growing on the ground, but not all species. Stems are centered and are either smooth, reticulated, dotted, or scabbed. Most are edible, and they include many delicious mushrooms. They comprise over 200 species; very few are toxic. And the results of a mistake are most often just an upset stomach and perhaps diarrhea. Their flavor ranges from excellent to sour or bitter. I often take a small bite of the raw bolete as a means of identification, rejecting bitter and sour specimens. Reactions differ between foragers. Follow this conservative advice, bearing in mind there are edible exceptions, until you are experienced. A very useful key to boletes is found here: www.mushroomexpert.com/boletes.html.

Caution:
• Eat young, fresh specimens.
• Avoid boletes with red or orange pore surfaces.
• Avoid boletes that have a yellow pore surface and bruise blue (the Red Cracked Bolete is the exception).
• Avoid (unless you are absolutely certain of identification) all orange-capped *Leccinum* species. *Leccinum* species are identified by "scabers" on their stems (see photo). You will miss a few edibles this way, but play it safe until you are expert and certain.
• Taste a small portion of a boletaceae—if it is bitter or sour do not eat.
• A few *Suillus* specimens may require removal of the sicky, slimy skin from the cap and stipe to avoid acrid taste and possible transient bowel problems. A bowel problem I have never experienced.

Bolete colors ranges from black and brown to yellow or red and various shades of the same. Caps are dry or slippery, smooth or scaly. Stems vary from solid to hollow and may be smooth or show veinlike ridges, dots (suillus), and tufts or scabers (leccinum). A partial veil and ring may be present or more often absent. Tubes show either a round or triangular pore. Younger boletes may have cotton plugs in their tubes. Pore color varies from white, yellowish, red, or green and may bruise to blue, blue green, blackish, or reddish. Spore-print color varies from olive to brown, black, pinkish, or yellowish.

Find Washington boletes in the spring, late summer, and throughout the fall. Eat them when they are young, firm, fresh, and insect-free (or free them from the insects).

Reticulated pattern of a bolete

Bolete that stains blue

Leccinum with scabers on stipe

Suillus with greasy dots on stem

King Bolete
Red Cracked Bolete
Admirable Bolete
Aspen Bolete
Western Painted Suillus
Suillus Ponderosus

King found near Mount St. Helens

KING BOLETE, CEP, PORCINI
Boletaceae (*Boletus edulis* Bull.)

Origin: Latin *boletus* means "mushroom"; edulis means "edible"

Season: Summer and fall—July–Sept

Identification: Large mushroom, 3"–10" in diameter, to 8" tall, a bun-shaped mushroom with a moist, smooth, and viscus surface (like a brown hamburger bun), sticky when wet. Color variable from biscuit brown, reddish brown, and paler; margins paler. Flesh is white and thick, greening and browning with age, often infested with worms, insects, and larvae. Small white tubes instead of gills, with the tube (pore) ends appearing to be stuffed with pith, first white in color and turning yellow, olive, or olive-yellow as it ages. Stipe is thick and sturdy, getting thicker toward the base. In Washington these mushrooms are solitary and scattered and occasionally in groups of 2 or 3. King boletes do not change color when touched or pinched!

Spore: Olive-brown, spore print brown

Habitat: I find king boletes around Mount Baker and its many trails, in the Cascades, and in the eastern mountain ranges of Washington—they're often in association there with ponderosa pine. They are widespread throughout Washington State. During July and Aug, look in recovering burn areas, along trails, and in campsites with 3'–15' spruce and new-growth pines. Often near streams with much dead timber on the ground in shade. Look along stream banks tucked under young conifers and the aprons of such and along edges of trails.

Look-alikes: See cautions in the opening of this chapter.

Edible: *B. edulis* is considered one of the safest wild mushrooms to pick for the table, but their color variability may confuse the novice. They are watery, so slice thin and sauté. Cook crisp with a strip or two of bacon. Eat or prepare as soon as possible; shelf life is short. Add to soups, pizza, and barbecue.

Medicinal: It is an antioxidant and antimicrobial food. A novel lectin from *B. edulis*, purified from the fruiting bodies, has potent antiproliferative effects on human cancer cells. *Boletus edulis* lectin (BEL) inhibits selectively the proliferation of several malignant cell lines and binds (inactivates) the neoplastic cell-specific T-antigen disaccharide (Bovi et al., 2011). *B. edulis* fruit bodies contain approximately 500 mg of ergosterol per 100 g of dried mushroom. A steroid derivative of ergosterol is antimicrobial and anti-inflammatory. Lectins in the mushroom stimulate cell division and are antiviral, inhibiting (in vitro) HIV. Antiviral activity extends to tobacco mosaic virus and *Vaccinia* species. Highest antioxidant activity appears to be in the edible cap. Ceps are one of the most important medicine sources of the Nahua people in the Mexican state of Tlaxcala.

Three kings and a queen

Caution: The mushroom chelates toxic heavy metals, such as selenium and cadmium. Avoid these mushrooms downstream of metal mines and in areas polluted by toxic tailings. If you fish for trout or salmon while foraging for mushrooms, follow the above advice—don't eat fish below mines and tailing spillovers.

Storage: Cook into dishes and then freeze. Slice thin and dry. The flavor (as with oyster mushrooms) intensifies with drying. Dry by stringing or in a food dryer or oven. Start oven temperature at 100°F with door open, dry between 120°F and 130°F until brittle and crisp; store in sealed jars. Reconstitute in hot water for 20 minutes or cook immediately in soups, stews, or in sauces such as pizza sauce. Use the soaking water in soups and side dishes, sauces and reductions, or store for later use.

Comments: Boletes are putrescent and break down into slimy, mushy, odorous masses after sitting too long unrefrigerated. Insects love this mushroom and almost instantly climb aboard. To ensure insect-free specimens, pick them in the morning, hopefully on the first day. This is often a large and abundant mushroom; take only what you can use.

RECIPE

Bolete Veggie Burgers

1 king bolete
Unsalted butter
Soy sauce
Balsamic vinegar
Garlic powder
Thyme
1 shallot

Cut a ½"-thick slice of the white flesh. Slice off pores and tubes. Place this slice in a plastic bag with a ¼ teaspoon of soy and ¼ teaspoon of balsamic vinegar. Shake the bag to thoroughly coat with the liquid, then sauté in butter with sliced shallot. Sprinkle on a pinch of garlic powder, a pinch of thyme, and pepper to taste, and put the sautéed bolete over a veggie burger. A buttered bun and cheese are optional.

Boletus chrysenteron HUGH SMITH

RED CRACKED BOLETE
Boletaceae *(Boletus chrysenteron* Bulliard preferred: *Xerocomellus chrysenteron* Bull. Sutara)

Origin: Boletus means "mushroom" and *chrysenteron* suggests "golden innards" or "gold intestine."
Season: Summer and fall in Washington
Identification: Medium-size mushroom, 1¼"–4" cap. Cap is convex to flat, velvety dark brown to olive brown to olive gray in color with reddish-tinged cracks displayed from margin. Tubes are yellow and stain blue when pinched. Tubes are sunken around stem's perimeter. Pores bright yellow and may display red here and there. Pores bruise blue. Stem is 1½"–2½" tall and ¼"–⅜" thick. Stem has no ring and stains blue. Stem is bicolor, yellow to reddish toward base, and does not bruise when cut. Flesh is white to yellow.
Spore: Spores are elliptical and smooth. Spore print olive-brown to olive colored.
Habitat: Found on mossy stream banks, under hardwoods, forest edges, along roadsides, often in residence with oaks and scrub oak, urban and suburban parks, paths
Look-alikes: Several to include *B. zelleri*, *B. subtomentosus*, and others; spores are indicative.
Edible: Edible
Comments: You will see this mushroom often, scattered or in groups. Color change in fruiting body pores (to blue) is helpful in identification. Not a particularly good-tasting bolete, providing a soft mouth feel and bland taste. Dr. Michael Beug, University of Washington, Burke Herbarium, warns not to eat when drinking alcohol to avoid gastrointestinal stress.
Recipe: First experience, slice thin and cook in butter and bacon until crisp.

Admirable bolete (Mount St. Helen's) HUGH SMITH

ADMIRABLE BOLETE
Boletaceae (*Aureoboletus mirabilis* Murr.)

Origin: *Mirabilis* is Latin for "wonderful" or "to marvel at."

Season: Sept, Oct, and into Dec

Identification: A dark and reddish-brown (maroon) bolete with a scaly, wooly cap (velvet-like) that flattens with maturity. At first cap is moist and then dry. Edge (margin) of cap is inrolled. Cap is 2½"–6" wide, at first convex and then nearly flat. Inner flesh is white and does not bruise blue*. Pores (tubes) are sunken near stalk and do not stain blue—pores yellow to olive-yellow. Stipe is 3"–6" tall and ⅜"–1¼" thick, dark brown in color, and webbed near top. It is club shaped and thicker at the base with a moist to dry feel. Stipe color is dark brown with sparse yellow streaks. Inner flesh is dingy pink or yellow.

  *I have harvested what I believed was *A. mirabilis* that did stain blue when bruised. Was it an exception? All other characteristics matched the species.

Spore: Olive-brown spore print. Individual spores elliptical and smooth.

Habitat: Prefers western hemlock, fir, and western red cedar and is found in duff or on dead and rotting conifers—unusual to find a bolete on dead and/or rotting wood, but this is an exception.

Look-alikes: Sand-preferring *Boletus projectellus* in conjunction with pine trees and sandy soil

Admirable bolete engulfed in *Hypomyces chrysospermus* white mold (found in Oregon)

Edible: The taste may be a bit sour.

Storage: Eat boletes as soon as possible as they do not store well.

Comments: *Hypomyces chrysospermus*, a white mold, can ruin the taste of this bolete. I find admirable boletes in and around Mount Adams and Mount St. Helens to name just a couple of habitats.

RECIPE

Mushroom Breakfast (versatile, simple recipe good with all mushrooms)

Bolete cap, thinly sliced
1 tbsp butter
1tbsp olive oil
2 tbsp water
1 tsp soy sauce
Onion, diced
Broccoli, thinly sliced
1 tbsp chopped poblano pepper
1 egg
1 slice sourdough bread, toasted

Slice the bolete cap thin (no pores), and sauté in a pan with butter, olive oil, and water. Splash in soy. Add onions, broccoli, and poblano pepper pieces. Sauté over medium heat for 4 minutes, then crack the egg over the top, cover the pan, and let the egg yolk harden in steam. Place over the sourdough toast, and garnish with a dollop of sour cream and 2 tablespoons salsa as a side.

LECCINUM SPECIES have spore-emitting tubes, and the stems are characterized by rigid projections called scabers, giving the stem a rough texture. It is a widely distributed genus in temperate latitudes, with over 75 species. Most are edible, but there have been gastrointestinal complaints from a red-capped species, perhaps *L. insigne*—accused, but not guilty until proven.

Aspen scaber-stalked bolete

ASPEN BOLETE, ASPEN SCABER STALK
Boletaceae (*Leccinum insigne*, Smith, Thiers, Watling)

Origin: *Leccinum* is Italian for "fungus," *insigne* Latin for "badge, flag, or distinguishing mark."
Season: Spring, summer, fall
Identification: This species is mycorrhizal (symbiotically) associated with aspen and birch, and that is critical to identification. The mushroom has a dry convex cap that is 1½"–6" wide, cap varies from reddish brown, rust-brown, to orangish brown. Cap goes from minutely scaly fibrils (fibrillose) to smooth with age. Stipe is 3"–5" tall and ⅜"–¾" thick, widening toward the base (as does *B. edulis*). Stipe is rough, white, with black scabers or scales (unlike *B. edulis*). Pores (tubes) are buff-white (off-white) aging to yellow-brown to olive-brown, and

stain yellow to yellow-brown when pinched. Pores are attached or descending the stipe. Flesh white, staining from purplish gray (violet) to black when pinched.

Spores: Spores are elliptical, yielding a yellow-brown spore print.

Habitat: Found under birch, aspen

Look-alikes: *Leccinum aurantiacum*, edible, which has a more orange cap and may be found in the same habitat, but more often with conifers.

Edible: Many foragers question the edibility of the species (see "Comments"): As with all boletes cook thoroughly. First experiences have left a few with an upset stomach. I have not experienced this, but I like to cook boletes crisp.

Medicinal: Like all boletaceae, a good source of fiber and high in potassium

Comments: *L. insigne* has numerous subspecies, so pinpointing identification is challenging. Also, *Leccinum* species have been implicated in toxic, allergic reactions. Being cautious, I cannot make a blanket statement about *L. insigne* as an edible mushroom. Once again, I have had no ill effect cooking it thoroughly, but others have suffered. For more see: www .mushroomexpert.com/leccinum.html.

RECIPE

Taco Pizza

10 corn tortillas
Taco mix
Water
1 lime
3 or 4 edible *Leccinum*
Saltless butter for sautéing
½ cup diced onion
Fresh cilantro
Hot sauce of your choice
Condiments: Salsa, sour cream, diced tomatoes, chopped lettuce

Sauté for 3 minutes mushrooms with onions, then add taco mix and water. Continue cooking to thicken. Heat tortillas to almost crisp, add mushroom taco mix and a squirt of lime, then load on salsa, diced tomatoes, lettuce, and dollop of sour cream. Color the cream with hot sauce and indulge.

SUILLIS is a large genus, widely dispersed, having members that may be found in Washington from fall to spring. Most are edible, taste and texture are good, but if you don't remove the slime, it may make you sick. They are identified by a number of general characteristics. Like the boletes, they have tubes, convex caps, and cylindrical stipes, with the lower end of the stipe in a few slightly bulging. They are slimy creatures (sorry!), but the caps are often slimy or sticky, and they have been given the generalized common monikers "slippery jacks," "slippery jills," sticky this, sticky that. Their caps can be peeled and the slimy skin scraped free from the stipes. They also have glandular dots on their stipes, not scabers. Their odor is of pine needles or fruity—like orange juice. They are medium-size. Caps are light brown. Boletes grow bigger, and bolete caps are darker brown, black, and red. *Suillus* species are linked to specific trees.

Suillus lakei HUGH SMITH

WESTERN PAINTED SUILLUS
Suillaceae (*Suillus lakei* [Murrill.] A. H. Smith and Thiers)

Origin: *Suillus* is Latin for "of swines." *Lakei* means "servant."
Season: Late summer to early fall
Identification: Mycorrhizal with Douglas fir primarily. The cap of this *Suillus* is up to 6" wide and slightly larger in perfect environments, near streams, deep shade, older Douglas firs. Cap edge (margin) is initially curved down, inward. Cap is dry, yellowish, reddish brown, or

orange buff, fading with age. Mushroom shows first with a convex cap and partial veil. Cap matures and flattens, veil leaves ring. The ring is scaly looking, of wooly tufts, and soon disappears, leaving a thin white ring remnant. Cap covered with scales or hairs toward the center, scales may be absent due to rain; on dry caps scales are prominent. Flesh of cap thick, yellow, and may or may not change color when cut or broken. If there is a color change, it is to pinkish red. The partial veil initially protecting the spore-emitting tubes bursts, and parts may hang from cap margin. Tubes are 0.2"–0.5" long and radially arranged, angular. Color of pore surface yellowish. Pores slowly stain brown to reddish brown or reddish clay when bruised or pinched. Stipe is 2.5"–5" and usually ½" to about 1" wide; above stipe is yellowish perhaps with reddish streaks and below ring similar to cap color. Stipe is cylindrical or slightly tapering toward end. Stipe typically lacks glandular dots. Stem in young specimens may stain bluish when cut.

Spores: Cinnamon-brown spore print

Habitat: Mycorrhizal association with Douglas fir. Look in campgrounds and along roads in conjunction with Douglas fir. Find them growing singly in grassy parklands studded with Douglas fir. Very common in Washington, occurring often with *S. caerulescens*, which has a whitish cap when young, changing to rosy red.

Look-alikes: Numerous look-alikes; Douglas fir is indicative of *S. lakei*. *S. spraguei* found in association with eastern white pine, *S. cavipes* and *S. ochraceoroseus* found with larch. *S. ponderosus* found with Douglas fir but has a gelatinous veil and slimy or sticky cap. *S. caerulescens* stains blue when stem is injured, broken, or cut, and older specimens are difficult to distinguish from *S. lakei*—at least for me—both are edible, but not choice.

Edible: Edible with variable reviews. You be the judge.

Medicinal: Petri dish tests show *S. lakei* extracts are antimicrobial, the action attributed to tannins and inherent alkaloids.

Comments: Four species: *S. lakei*, *S. caerulescens*, *S. imitates*, and *S. ponderosus* (next) are all difficult to distinguish and can occur in the same location. *S. imitates* and *S. ponderosus* are rare in Washington. None of these species are poisonous. They are not all pleasant to the palate, and rarely, a person may have an allergic reaction.

Suillus ponderosus HUGH SMITH

SUILLUS PONDEROSUS
Suillaceae (*Suillus ponderosus* A. H. Smith and Thiers)

NOTE: I have never found this species while foraging for mushrooms in Washington. There is, however, anecdotal evidence that it has been found in Washington State. This mushroom's typical habitat is California. So read carefully and take up the challenge—see if you can find this mushroom in Washington.

Origin: *Suillus* is Latin for "of swines." *Ponderosus* means "heavy" or "brutus" in Latin.

Season: Fall through winter

Identification: Mycorrhizal with Douglas fir growing on the wood and ground. It has a gelatinous yellow to orange partial veil that tears free after emerging and leaves a ring on upper stipe. Ring or ring remnant on stipe is brown to reddish brown. Cap orange-brown to light brownish yellow with hint of orange. Often paler toward margin. Smooth cap that is viscid (sticky, greasy) and even slimy when wet. Flesh yellowish to yellow white and color does not change when cut or torn. Stipe is cylindrical, solid, and may be slightly swollen as it descends, dingy white to cream and darker below as it ages. Tube ends have orange-tinted ring. They are short, decurrent, yellow to grayish yellow. Pores somewhat angular and the same color as tubes—they darken (brown) when bruised. No distinctive odor or taste.

Spores: Spore print brown

Habitat: Found singly and gregarious in association with pines, specifically and primarily Douglas fir in the habitats where they are found in Washington—perhaps the Okanagan Valley and Puget Sound.

Look-alikes: Found in the same environments are *Suillus lakei*, *S. imitates*, *S. caerulescens*, and *S. grevellei*, all mushrooms associated with larch, Douglas fir, or other pines.

Edible: Edible and better tasting when cap skin and stipe slime is removed.

Medicinal: No medical or dietary information currently available

Comments: *Suillus* mushrooms in the fall inherit the forest and can be found in large numbers in numerous habitats. I have even found them in lowlands up to their necks in water. The feel may be discouraging, but go ahead and indulge yourself.

Recipe: Alas, as mentioned I have not found this mushroom, but according to others it is there. To eat edible *Suillus* species, remove the sticky, slimy skin and the veil and scrape the stipe. For more *Suillus* and *Boletus* recipes: http://foragerchef.com.

RECIPE

Suillus Meatloaf

1 pound ground sirloin
1 pound chopped *Suillus* caps
1 cup dried bread crumbs
½ large (½ cup diced) sweet onion
1 cup milk
1 egg
1 cup ketchup
1 tbsp Worcestershire sauce
1 tbsp balsamic vinegar
1 tbsp dried parsley
1 tbsp garlic powder
Salt and pepper to taste

Make a ketchup glaze for the top of the meatloaf with ¾ cup ketchup, a tablespoon of Worcestershire sauce, and 1 tablespoon of balsamic vinegar. Sauté mushrooms in 1 tablespoon each of unsalted butter and olive oil. Then fold in and mix all the ingredients with your clean hands. Pat meatloaf flat in a loaf pan. Pour over the ketchup glaze. Place in a preheated oven at 350°F and bake for 55 minutes.

5   Puffballs

Gem-studded puffball

Puffballs are saprobes that begin to appear in the summer and continue showing through the fall. They are round, oval, or pear shaped and found across the continent in hardwood and coniferous forests, lawns, gardens, and parks. They range from small to large (1"–24" in diameter), whitish to brown (but never green, red, orange, or pink), and are edible when fresh and not colored by spores. Puffballs encompass several genera, to include *Calvatia*, *Lycoperdon*, and *Calbovista*. Larger ones are easy to identify. Most grow on top of the ground without a distinctive stem, others attach to dead wood (stumps and trees) and may have a stemlike extension to their body. Puffballs produce spores in a stomach-like spherical fruiting body called a gasterothecium. In time, the puffball either develops a vent or it dries and splits, releasing the spores. Larger species produce billions of spores. And with all that, their success continues. I find the smaller ones tasty. *Caution:* Be certain to read the section on puffball look-alikes on page 71.

> Western Giant Puffball
> Giant Puffball
> Gem Puffball
> Pear-Shaped Puffball

Feed the crowd, *C. booniana*. HUGH SMITH

WESTERN GIANT PUFFBALL
Lycoperdaceae (*Calvatia booniana* A. H. Smith)

Origin: *Calvatia* is Latin meaning "bald." *Booniana* is "land of Boone," named after William Boone, the first president of the College of Idaho.

Season: Summer and fall

Identification: *Big!* Can be seen from a moving car (screech!). Large soccer ball shape (and even larger), growing alone or gregarious, sometimes in a fairy ring. Inner flesh, the gleba, or spore-producing area of the mushroom, is first white and then darkens as it ages and spores mature—a distinctive mushroom with a patterned skin.

Spores: Olive-brown, round. The total number of spores produced by a single, average-size giant puffball *C. booniana* estimated at around 7 trillion.

Habitat: Drier open areas of Washington such as the steppes, often with sage and juniper. Also found along forest fringes and lower meadows under trees and shrubs, and often in lawns. I have found it in a city park.

Look-alikes: Size sets it apart. It is the biggest puffball in Washington. *C. gigantea*, found east of the Rockies, is often bigger. There is another *Calvatia* growing along the Pacific Coast that is more *C. gigantea*–like. All are edible, an acquired taste.

Edible: Peel skin, slice thin, bread or dust in flour, and sauté. This is the quickest way to prepare the mushroom.

Storage: When sliced in thin sections and dried, this mushroom becomes lighter than air. You can freeze the sections after drying, or store them in a sealed container. Cooked mushroom may be stored in the freezer. Texture is mushy.

Comments: I wanted to relieve a city park of one of these eye-catching mushrooms. There it was with lovers and children all around. *Who is the guy stealing our big beautiful mushroom. Let's get him.* The next year the park was pimpled white with these large mushrooms and the city had them all removed. *C. booniana* can be found in the same place for several years. The largest *booniana* puffball I ever found was in the park across from the Buffalo Bill Museum in Cody, Wyoming.

Recipe: Slice thin, cut away thick patterned skin, dust in cake flour (fine and light), then dip into 2 beaten raw eggs (try duck eggs). Sprinkle on a little more flour and sauté on medium heat until coating is crusty and brown.

C. gigantea south coast of Washington and into California

GIANT PUFFBALL
Lycoperdaceae (*Calvatia gigantea* [Batsch ex Pers.] Lloyd)

Origin: *Calvatia* means "bald" and *gigantea* means "giant"
Season: Late summer, fall
Identification: Grows solitary or closely dispersed and is about the size of a soccer ball, even larger. Flesh is white, and a thick white to off-white skin protects flesh. A *Calvatia gigantea* specimen was found that was 5′ in diameter and weighed 40 pounds.
Spores: Brown
Habitat: There is a similar or same species found in coastal areas of Washington in association with hardwoods, shady areas, and open areas.
Look-alikes: See *C. booniana*.
Edible: Cut open flesh to determine if it is gill-free and white inside, then cut flesh in ¼ slices, dip in whipped egg, dredge in cake flour, and sauté.
Medicinal: In traditional Chinese medicine, puffballs are considered anticancer. The anticancer agent calvacin has been isolated from young fruit bodies and cultures of *C. gigantea*, as well as from a few other puffball species. In vitro it has inhibited tumor cells. *M. pyriformis*, the pear-shaped puffball, may aid or induce sleep. All puffball spores are styptic wound sealants. Calvacin from *Calvatia* species in vivo tests on mouse, rat, and hamster cells demonstrated antitumor activity in 14 of the tumor types. However, clinical/animal testing revealed numerous side effects, including anorexia, acute liver failure, muscle inflammation, and bleeding from the lungs (Wang et al., 2014).

Storage: As with *C. booniana*, cook into dishes and freeze, or slice large puffballs thinly and dry in a food dryer; powder the end product and add to soups, stews, and dishes improved by a mushroom flavor. Powdered mushroom stores in sealed glass jar (1 year).

Comments: *Calvatia gigantea* has been used traditionally by the Cree as a styptic wound dressing. A dried slice of the mushroom placed over a wound contracts tissue and reduces bleeding. After initial sopping of blood, place a new slice over wound as a dressing. Native Americans used the soft, white inner flesh to remove objects from the eye. Blackfoot drank the spores to stem internal bleeding. The Haisla Nation thought the spores of *Calvatia* poisonous. Anthropologists found puffballs in grave sites over 2,000 years old. Traditionally, *C. gigantea* spores were used to treat ear infections—spores are blown into the ear using a paper cone. The Masai mix spores of *Calvatia* into milk and drink it to relieve stomachaches. Nepalese villagers used a water-wetted spore paste from dried puffballs to treat wounds and abrasions on pack animals. In Mexico, puffballs are used to treat insect bites and stings.

Recipe: When sliced and dried the mushroom takes on the weight of helium. It wants to float from your hand. Corral it, put it in a ziplock bag, and crush it into powder. Use the powder to impart a mushroom flavor to soups, stews, and sauces—about a tablespoon of powder to 12 ounces of broth. Powdered puffballs will not completely dissolve—keep stirring.

Lycoperdon perlatum

GEM PUFFBALL, DEVIL'S SNUFF
Agaricaceae (*Lycoperdon perlatum* Persoon: Persoon)

Origin: *Lycoperdon* derived from Greek to mean roughly "wolf fart." *Perlatum* meaning "ample," pertaining to the number of spines.

Season: Late summer, fall

Identification: White, turban-shaped (like an upside-down pear) mushroom 1"–2½" wide and 1½"–3" tall. Apical spore dispersal pore central on top. Mushroom tapering to a stalklike base when base is present, but when young the base is not evident. Pyramidal spines cover top down upper third of stalk-like base. Spines may be broken off, leaving a weblike scar. Flesh best when young and white, and turns greenish brown and less desirable with age.

Spores: Round spores white to green tinged to reddish brown

Habitat: Disturbed ground along roadsides, trails, gardens, fields, and grassy clearings in the woods

Look-alikes: May be confused as a poisonous amanita egg. Always cut open and make certain there are no developing gills inside.

Edible: Considered choice by many, but must be young and white throughout. Slice thin and fry crisp.

Medicinal: Laboratory in vitro studies show this is an antimicrobial mushroom; active chemistry includes lycoperic acid and various sterols.

Storage: Slice in half and dry in a food dryer, or sauté slices and freeze.

Comments: Found throughout the 2 seasons after rain. Size varies with substrate and local moisture. Found singly or 2 or 3 close together.

RECIPE

Chili Cook-Off Winner

If you want to win the next chili cook-off, chop these mushrooms and sauté with chopped bacon until crisp, then stir bits into sour cream and put the sour cream over your best chili recipe.

M. pyriformis spewing spores from a dead tree

PEAR-SHAPED PUFFBALL, STUMP PUFFBALL
Lycoperdaceae (*Morganella pyriformis* [Schaeff.] Kreisel & D. Kruger)

Origin: *Morganella*, proper noun, English surname. *Pyriformis* means "pear shaped."
Season: Summer, fall
Identification: Small, round or pear-shaped puffball, 1"–2" and as tall or slightly taller. Color of "pear body" is off-white to tannish brown, bearing small white spines that fall off by maturity. Mature fruiting body disperses spores from a top-side central vent. Foot or base of mushroom appears pinched and is attached to logs and wood with thick mycelium, called rhizomorphs. Inner flesh white when young, aging to dark olive-brown when mature.
Spores: Brown to dark olive-brown staining the inner flesh
Habitat: Found in forests on dead and decaying wood
Look-alikes: Other puffballs are similar, but pear shape and spines are distinctive, found on wood. Similar to *Lycoperdon perlatum* but darker in outer skin color.
Edible: If you are not certain of the species of puffball you are eating, consult an expert. Prepare only white and densely fruited puffballs. Use fresh or slice thin and dry immediately. Dried puffballs have all the mass of helium-filled balloons. Pulverize the dried mushroom into powder and stir the powder into dishes to impart a mushroom flavor. Fresh puffballs are sliced, breaded, and sautéed or deep-fried. The flavor is good, enhanced by the addition of fresh ginger and tamari or soy sauce; the texture is mushy.
Medicinal: As with other puffballs, spores are used as a styptic to stem bleeding.

Storage: Cook into dishes and freeze, or slice large puffballs thinly and dry in a food dryer; powder the end product and add to soups, stews, and dishes requiring a mushroom flavor. Give powder to friends and have them experiment.
Comments: Use dried puffballs as tinder for starting fires. Smoldering, this mushroom may be effective for shooing bees when hand-extracting wild honey; the smoke appears to sedate the bees.

RECIPE

Panko Smash

Smash smaller puffballs flat with a knife or wooden paddle, dust with flour or panko, and fry crisp. Slide into a sandwich, lather with mayo, dill pickle, sliced tomato, and lettuce.

TOXIC PUFFBALL LOOK-ALIKES (INEDIBLE)

Caution: Not edible. Always slice the puffball mushroom in half to check for gills (or what may be the development of a gilled mushroom). Evidence of gills means it is not a puffball and is possibly a poisonous amanita in the egg stage. Even the ephemeral hint of gills indicates an amanita. Do not eat it!

The pigskin poison puffball (*Scleroderma citrinum*, Pers) and other sclerodermas look like edible puffballs. *Scleroderma citrinum* is yellow-brown with a tough, thick, and warty skin. At maturity it is purplish and hard inside. It grows to 1"–4" in diameter and has a topside vent emitting blackish-brown spores. Avoid these mushrooms.

Toxic amanita puffball-like "egg"

Scleroderma citrinum, toxic puffball look-alike

6   Morels and Inedible False Morels

Grill a morel, place it on a taco.

Morels are considered the prime rib of mushrooms. It is perhaps the most sought-after edible wild mushroom, and for a few, all other edible mushrooms are either unknown or "poisonous." They are found throughout the United States, Mexico, Canada, and as far north as the Arctic Circle. In Washington they show as early as March in warmer, wetter valleys and as late as July in recent burnouts at high altitudes, exceeding 6,200 feet. Measure your start by latitude and altitude.

Morels do not have conventional mushroom gills, tubes, or teeth. They are asco-mycetes; that is, they are spore shooters rather than spore droppers; and their convoluted, brain-like shape facilitates this type of dispersal. Morels are mycor-rhizal partners with trees to include conifers (conifer burnouts), poplars, apple trees, madrone, black cottonwood (river bottoms), honeysuckle, elm, and ash. Look for them along trails and in campgrounds, on gentle slopes, and in shaded areas of downed trees. Keep in mind they can be found in fairly open areas and in deep shade. Fence rows bordering woods often produce. Begin your search when apple trees bloom and lilacs flush.

Rule of thumb: Black morels have dark ridges and lighter pits; yellow morels have lighter ridges and darker pits.

Black Morel
Yellow Morel
Gray Morel
Half Free Cap Morel
False Morels

Clockwise from top left: Gray morel found at 7,000 feet in late June; black morel with dark edges, lighter pits; basket of yellow morels; the free cap morel is considered edible but has toxic look-alikes. Don't mistake this edible mushroom for a *Verpa* false morel. Like the free cap, the cap of the *Verpa* is delicate and easily pulls off. The *Verpa* is attached at the pinnacle of the stem, and *Verpa* caps are wrinkled and not pitted. Color may be similar.

MORELS

Morchellaceae:
Black morel (*Morchella brunnea*, Kuo 2012)
Yellow morel (gray when young) (*Morchella esculentoides*)
Gray morel (*Morchella tomentosa*, Kuo)
Half free cap morel (*Morchella populiphila*, Kuo, Carter, Moore)

Origin: *Morchel* is German meaning "fungus." *Tomentosa* means "covered with hairs."

Season: Spring as measured by latitude and altitude, earlier at lower latitudes and later at higher altitudes. Found from Mar to late June in Washington. Spring as measured by blooming apple blossoms.

Identification: Morchella is a large and complex genus. Members of the genus are fairly simple to identify—it gets more difficult to get to species. With help you can. One good resource is www.mushroomexpert.com/morchellaceae.html.

True morels belong to the genus *Morchella*, whereas false morels are *Verpas* and *Gyromitras*, and elfin saddles are *Helvella*. Of the four morels described here:

Black morels are found under oaks and other hardwoods including madrone and possibly conifers. The species was identified and named by Kuo in 2012. It is similar to the black morel of the eastern United States but smaller. Conical cap with vertically arranged ridges and pits. Ridges are black and pits lighter, brown to tan. Stipe is hollow and as long as the cap is tall. Base of stipe slightly swollen.

Yellow morels, in contrast, start out gray and mature to yellow with a full body of pits, and ridges of different shapes and sizes. Cap and stems are hollow. They can exceed 10" in height, but are typically in the 3"–6" range. Yellow morels are domestic, found in urban settings: parks, along bike trails, and in conjunction with cottonwoods (river bottoms), ash, apple, and pear trees, and along the edges of campgrounds.

Gray morels have a brain-like outer appearance—ridged and pitted—with pits arranged in columns or laddered. Cap and stem are hollow in the middle and take the form of a jester-shaped cap that tapers. Stems darken with age and can be blackish at maturity. Mushroom ranges from 2" to 8" in height. In general, morels love rich soils with a lot of humus (or ash) and rotting fallen trees and stumps. These are mushrooms of the spring, and the mushrooms of conifer forest burnouts. Their appearance occurs in spring, the timing of which varies by latitude and altitude.

Half free cap morel caps are small, 1"–1½" wide, and proportionally the stem is long, up to 6" overall. The bottom half of the cap is free from the stem, hanging as if a skirt. When cut in half, the attachment is evident.

Spores: Cream to yellow colored

Habitat: Morels are found in almost all Washington ecosystems, valleys, mountains, coastal areas, and river bottoms, preferring some exposure to light but not dry areas. Hugh Smith finds morels in pear orchards. Gray morels are professionally harvested and commonly found in markets. They are found especially in conifer burnouts. Half free caps, more commonly found in Oregon, may be found in conjunction (under) black cottonwoods, *Populus trichocarpa*, growing in river bottoms.

Look-alikes: *Verpas* and *Gyromitras*: *Gyromitra* and false morels look similar to edible morels but have grotesque folds and are saddle shaped and brain shaped without hollow stems. Certain *Verpa* species can be confused with the edible free cap morel (see photo). Like *Gyromitra*, *Verpas* do not present the open hollow body and stem of edible morels.

Edible: A much sought-after and versatile edible mushroom, use morels fresh or dried in savory entrees, egg dishes, with game and fowl, in soups, chowders, pastas, infused in cheese, on toast . . . I am just warming up. Morels are delicious in all dishes where mushrooms improve taste: omelets, frittatas, pizza, pasta, burgers, veggie burgers (sauté with wild stinging nettle, asparagus, and red bell pepper). Sauté the first bunch of the season in a pinch of butter and olive oil and serve on buttered sourdough toast points. Delicious with eggs, beef, venison, cheese, and duck.

Medicinal: In China, morels are considered an immune-modulating food, toning the stomach and intestines and opening channels regulating energy throughout the body—good for reducing phlegm and indigestion. Research suggests eating morels might be antitumor and anti-inflammatory, at least in animal models (Nitha, Meera, and Janardhanan, 2007). At just 3 micrograms per milliliter, morel polysaccharides stimulate immune-system response initiated in the mucosal immune system interface (Duncan et al., 2002; Lull, Wichers, and Savelkoul, 2005). Ethanol extract of morels inhibits chronic and acute inflammation and prevents the growth of solid cancer tumors (Nitha, Meera, and Janardhanan, 2007). The polysaccharide (complex sugars) fraction appears to stimulate the immune system, providing enhanced immune protection.

Storage: Brush morels clean, cook in dishes, and freeze (cook frozen, don't thaw), or dry and store in canning jars. Try pickling them. Freeze fresh and whole for up to a month.

Caution: Eat morels in moderation. One study reported 146 patients presented gastrointestinal syndrome and 129 presented neurologic syndrome. Gastrointestinal and other neurological symptoms were also present (ocular/vision disorders, paresthesia, drowsiness/confusion, and muscle disorders). These patients frequently ingested a large quantity of morels. Confusion with *Gyromitra esculenta* (false morels) was ruled out (Saviuc, 2010, May). To denature the gastrointestinal irritants, *always cook morels thoroughly.*

Comments: In southern Poland this mushroom is linked with the devil or the devil's work. German folklore espouses that the devil condemned a wrinkled old woman to the existence of the mushroom. To this day, it is an insult to call a German woman a "morel." Morels prefer a little sunlight, such as along fence lines and trail sides on the west or north side, in areas without high winds and in open burn areas. In a lowland marsh near me, the water

---

RECIPE

Morels in a Hurry

Morels are great sautéed by themselves in olive oil, butter, and/or with bacon.

Try them whole or sliced in half; sauté halves (see tip below), cool, then stuff the cooked halves with mozzarella cheese (a bit tedious but worth it). Next, on a baking tray, broil for 2 minutes until mozzarella browns (watch closely). A drop or two of Sriracha or Tapatío adds a palate-pleasing zing. Serve as an appetizer.

Also, consider lightly breaded and fried morels added to venison or buffalo burger—sensational.

Sautéed morels on toasted sourdough bread, lathered with a thin layer of mayonnaise, are simple, elegant, and delicious. Top with a thin slice of tomato.

and elevation keep things cooler for longer into the spring; there, the morels come a week or so later. I have seen morels picked in burnouts at 7,000 feet in Washington; the higher you go, the later in the season you will find them. In the United States, starting fires to stimulate morel growth is a crime with severe penalties.

Tip: When cooking morels in a pan with butter, moisture will leave the whole mushrooms, forming a milky bath in the pan. Continue cooking the morels on low heat until this milky (watery) liquid evaporates. When gone, the mushrooms are done and taste like steak.

Verpa species are best avoided.

Gyromitra—chambered and not hollow

FALSE MORELS—INEDIBLE
Discinaceae (*Gyromitra* species) and Morchellaceae (*Verpa* species)

Caution: *Not edible.* False morels, *Gyromitra* species, are included here as a potentially toxic look-alike. Avoid this mushroom. Other guides suggest that thorough cooking denatures the toxin, but don't believe it!

Origin: *Gyrus* is Latin for "convoluted folds of the brain."

Season: Spring

Identification: *Gyromitra* are convoluted throughout and more extremely shaped than morels—as if in a science-fiction movie in which they were nuked and came out scary look-ing. The Doctrine of Signatures suggests, whether always reliable or not, if it looks danger-ous, it very well is dangerous. Caps are weird—wavy, lobed, pitted, ridged, saddle shaped, and convoluted. Cap color varies from reddish and reddish brown to very dark brown and occasionally yellowish brown. The caps are also more densely full than morels, and stems are not hollow. Whereas morels are completely hollow, *Gyromitra* are not—they have pock-ets but are not completely hollow.

Spores: Spore colors similar to cap colors: brown to dark brown and variable to reddish brown, yellowish, and orangish brown

Habitat: Found in the same places as edible morels at the same time and even earlier

7   Jelly Fungi

Jelly fungus

Jelly mushrooms are amorphous, gelatinous mushrooms (jellylike in texture and/ or appearance) that come in many sizes, shapes, and colors. They are saprobes found on dead, decaying wood. Of these jelly fungi, wood ears are tastiest. Most others are tasteless or considered inedible, but they are always a delight to behold and worthy members of an ever-expanding repertoire of your fungi knowledge.

Wood Ears
Alpine Jelly Cone (Gumdrops)
Fan-Shaped Jelly Fungus

Wood ear is often found on rotting elder wood.

WOOD EARS
Auriculariaceae (*Auricularia auricula-judae* (Bull.) J. Schröt.)

Origin: *Auricula* is Latin for "external ear."

Season: Begin your search in the spring while morel hunting.

Identification: Ear-shaped or cuplike saprobe, brown to grayish black, to 4" wide plus or minus, with folds resembling those forming the pinna of a human ear. Underside is a lighter shade that is more reddish brown to gray black, wavy, smooth, velvety, fine hairs. It is cartilaginous or rubbery to the touch, thin fleshed, with irregular folds (veins), and grows in groups on dead branches, typically elder.

Spore: It emits a white to off-white to yellowish sausage-shaped spore, and the print is white.

Habitat: A difficult find for me. Found in woods, fringes of woods, and edges of streams, ponds, and lakes; grows on wood (on disintegrating, rotted wood) that can be shredded with your fingers—many sources mention elder trees as a preferred habitat. Although available for several months, we find it rarely, or rather accidentally, stumbling over it.

Look-alikes: A *Gyromitra* could be mistaken for a wood ear, but *Gyromitras* grow on the ground and not dead limbs and their flesh is brittle. A few cup fungi look similar, but they also grow on the ground and are brittle, not flexible.

Edible: Wash thoroughly, then add to Asian stir-fry, or simply sauté in butter—an interesting chewy texture and surprisingly good taste—great in sauces cooked with wild leeks, thickened with sour cream, and served over toast. The fungus is a popular ingredient in hot-and-sour soup.

Medicinal: *A. auricula-judae* was a folk medicine treatment for sore throats, sore eyes, and jaundice. It is astringent and also used in Ghana as a blood tonic. Modern research into possible medical applications variously concluded that *A. auricula-judae* is anticoagulant, anti-inflammatory, antitumor, hypoglycemic, and has cholesterol-lowering properties (Luo et al., 2011).

The mushroom is anti-inflammatory, antioxidant, and anti-thrombotic, and inhibits platelet aggregation. Simply grow or forage for the mushroom and then eat it (Powell, 2014). Recent investigations strongly suggest *A. auricula-judae* polysaccharides show an antidiabetic hypoglycemic effect, reducing plasma glucose, insulin, urinary glucose, and food intake (Yuan et al., 1998).

Caution: Dr. Dale Hammerschmidt, a hematologist from Minnesota, linked eating wood ear mushrooms to bleeding and its antiplatelet-aggregating activity. People on blood thinners should consult their physicians. *A. auricula-judae* may possess a possible antifertility agent and should not be taken by pregnant or lactating women or those planning to conceive.

Storage: Wood ears are best stored dried and kept in sealed jars, or frozen in cooked dishes and double-wrapped.

Comments: I found wood ears the first time while searching for morels; they were growing on small lengths of rotting wood (probably elder), and I found them throughout the spring and summer. The best time to hunt and taste them is after a soaking rain. Folklore suggests this fungus emerged for the first time in the shape of an ear on the site where Judas died.

RECIPE

Wild Leeks, Daylily Buds, and Wood Ears

Wood ears are readily available in Asian markets. They are typically dried. They're a versatile addition to o'soba, miso soup, and stir-fry.

2 tbsp balsamic vinegar
2 tbsp butter
⅓ cup water
1 cup wood ear mushrooms
1 cup daylily buds or flowers without pistils and stamens
⅓ cup chopped wild leeks
1 tsp chopped fresh Asian ginger
1 tbsp soy sauce

Whether found in the wild or purchased at the farmer's market, wood ears are delicious sautéed in butter and balsamic vinegar with wild leeks and daylily buds. The leeks will have lost their leaves by the time the lily buds or lily flowers are available, so use the leek bulb. Slice the cup of mushrooms into strips. Chop the leeks. Remove pistils and stamens from the flowers. Then add 2 tablespoons of butter to a sauté pan plus 2 table-spoons of balsamic vinegar, and ⅓ cup of water. Stir in ginger, leeks, daylilies, and wood ears. Sauté until leeks soften. Blend in 1 tablespoon of soy and serve as a side dish or omelet stuffing.

Guepiniopsis alpina

ALPINE JELLY CONE, GOLDEN JELLY CONE, GUMDROPS
Dacrymycetaceae (*Guepiniopsis alpina* [Tracy & Earle] Brasf)

Origin: *Guepiniopsis* translates roughly to "knowledge," and *alpinus* means "alpine."
Season: Spring and other seasons as moisture allows
Identification: The golden jelly or alpine jelly cone is a western jelly fungus, conical, bell shaped or fan shaped, gelatinous, that is found hanging from a point (pendant-like) in groups on dead conifers in Washington. Fruiting bodies are yellow to orange; small 0.16"–0.3" (4–8 mm); bell-, pendant-, cone-, or fan-shaped; often hanging from a single point of attachment like a gumdrop. Surface dries hard to yellow-brown or reddish orange. Outer surface wrinkled, finely hairy; inner surface smooth.
Spores: Sausage-shaped, yellow spores
Habitat: Conifer forests, on dead or downed pines and firs, saprophytic, in moist, cool, shady areas up to 9,000 feet—often just as the spring thaw uncovers the logs
Look-alikes: Cup fungi are brittle.
Edible: Claimed to be edible mushroom but is bland to tasteless
Medicinal: As folk medicine, it was (is) eaten to treat headaches.
Comments: Found while tripping through long-dead pines
Recipe: Not a significant food source because of its small size

Spathularia growing from a crack in treated pier boards

FAN-SHAPED JELLY FUNGUS, EAR FUNGUS (CHINESE)
Dacrymycetaceae (*Dacryopinax spathularia* [Schwein] GW Martin) Syn. (*Cantharellus spathularius*, Schwein)

Origin: *Dacry* means "tear," and *pinax* means "likeness," thus "like a tear." *Spathul* means "blade" or "spadelike."

Season: Summer or fall (in Washington, July–Dec) after considerable wetness and high humidity

Identification: Tiny, erect saprophytic jelly fungus, orange to yellow-orange, ½"–1" (0.5–2 cm) tall, and typically half as wide. Spade- or spatula-shaped fruiting body on rounded stalk, often described as fan shaped. Ephemeral, wilting as the day progresses to reinstate itself by morning—grows erect and in clusters in cracks of decaying pine board.

Spores: Translucent (hyaline)

Habitat: In the cracks of decorticated (bark removed) wood. Boards of tree houses and playground decking, plus older pier (dock) slats or boards frequently have the mushroom growing in colonies from the cracks in the wood. Found from coast to coast, even in chemically treated boards.

Look-alikes: There are several species in the genus; shape, saprophytic substrate, and size are indicative.

Edible: With this caveat: The mushroom will grow from treated boards that may be toxic.

Medicinal: Chinese medicine

Storage: Eat fresh and immediately. Asians dry the mushroom, but who has the time for such a small morsel of fungus?

Comments: The mushroom is often included in the Chinese Buddhist vegetarian dish Buddha's Delight, or Lo Han Jai. It features several mushrooms including wood ear mushrooms, 18 to 20 nuts, seeds, noodles, and vegetables. See recipe: www.dinneratthezoo.com/buddhas-delight/.

8   Coral Fungi

Crown coral

These mushrooms have the shape, variety, and color of marine corals, hence the name. A few grow in clumps in fingerlike projections, and others are club-shaped and singular. A few are edible and others are toxic. There are over 600 varieties of coral fungi. There are tan, off-white or yellowish, and purple varieties mimicking aquatic corals. Coral mushrooms are also found in bright-pink and orange-red varieties. They frequently come in bright, highly recognizable colors—yellow and pink for example. They feel rubbery to the touch, then become hard and tough as they age. Here are two edibles to start you on your journey.

Spring Coral
Crown Coral

Ramaria magnipes emerging

SPRING CORAL, YELLOW CORAL
Gomphaceae (*Ramaria magnipes*, Mar & Stuntz)

Origin: *Ramaria*, meaning "many-branched," and *magnipes*, meaning "great foot."
Season: Spring, summer
Identification: A medium to large coral mushroom 2"–6" wide and 2"–6" tall. Yellowish tips rise from thick whitish stipes (stem) that branch several times. First branches are thick, from 1" to 1½", then subsequent branches thinner, less than half of the thickness of primary branches. Fibrous flesh is tough and bendable when dry (older). Odor and taste undistinctive. Stipe flesh does not bruise pale yellow, and mushroom heads are pale yellow to pale orange-yellow, cauliflower-like, more or less like yellow broccoli head. Tips age to brown.
Caution: Avoid coral mushrooms with gelatinous bases, or bases or coral-like tops that bruise brown and/or taste bitter.
Spore: Cylindrical shaped
Habitat: Found in coniferous forests, east slope of Cascades, and farther east in montane environments. Look in the spring and winter in Washington. When fresh, *R. magnipes* may be mostly buried in pine duff and appear as tufts of cauliflower emerging from the pine floor.
Look-alikes: *Ramaria rasilispora* var. *scatesiana* is similar but appears lighter in color and is also edible. *Ramaria formosa* has yellow tips and coral-pink stems that mature to pink and is poisonous. And *R. rasilispora* var. *rasilispora* is similar and edible.

Edible: Fibrous texture, best when young and just emerging from conifer duff. I have had this served raw, but a few people have reactions, so first try it thoroughly cooked.

Comments: Leave the trail, cut across country through the pines in the spring of the year and you will be rewarded. Often found in the summer and fall too.

RECIPE

Ramaria Tempura

These mushrooms go well in a stir-fry with Chinese vegetables or as Japanese tempura with shrimp tempura and broccoli tempura (for contrast). Buy tempura mix at an Asian market or make your own. Here's my recipe.

5 oz. each of cake (or pastry) flour and white rice flour
12 oz. club soda (seltzer water)
1 tbsp rice wine or vodka (optional)
Cup of ice
Frying oil (4 qt. pan with 2 or at most 3 quarts of oil)
2 eggs
¼ lb. mushrooms

Mix the 2 dry flours in one bowl. In a second bowl whip the 2 eggs with 12 oz. of club soda and the tablespoon of alcohol (wine or vodka). Add the cup of ice to the blended eggs, soda water, and wine. Next add flour mixture to eggs (save about a ⅓ of the dry flour mix for coating the mushrooms). Add flour by hand, punch in with fingers, leaving a lumpy mix with patches of dry flour. In the meantime, in a 4-quart/deep pan, bring 2 quarts of oil to 360°F. Then return to the flour-egg mixture and stir until runny and lumpy. Next, powder the mushrooms (or dredge) with dry flours. Dip the mushrooms in the flour-egg mixture, sprinkle a bit of flour on top, and deep-fry in the pan—about 2 minutes plus or minus until golden brown. Frying in less oil gives mixed results (not as fluffy), but either way, your guests will be pleased. Cook in small batches without crowding. For best results keep oil between 360°F and 375°F.

Crown coral

CROWN CORAL
Auriscalpiaceae (*Artomyces pyxidata* (Persoon: Fries). Doty = *Clavicorona pyxidata*, Fries, Doty)

Origin: Latin *auriscalpium* roughly means "ear pick."

Season: Summer to late fall

Identification: Crown coral is a saprobe, found primarily on rotting willow, poplar, and aspen wood. The shape and points (typically 4) on the tips of the numerous branches are distinctive, crown-like—the entire mushroom is 2"–5" tall. Color is pallid to dull cream, pale yellowish, tan to pale pink. Basidia and basidiospores are produced on the surface of the branches. Taste is peppery when raw and nondescript when cooked. Branches rise from the fruiting body base. Flesh is white, texture firm to tough.

Spores: Colorless, spore print white

Habitat: On decaying wood throughout North America; widely available in late summer through the fall

Look-alikes: *Clavulina cristata* is similar but branch tips are pointed, as if toothed. And *C. avellanea*, found on coniferous wood in Washington, has stems (branches) that are grayish brown with pale tips that soon turn brown with age.

Edible: I like to sauté the mushroom in oil for a couple minutes, then add water, cover, and let simmer until tender—a survival food.

Medicinal: The sesquiterpenes pyxidatols A–C, tsuicoline E, and omphadiol of this mushroom are anti-inflammatory and antiseptic.

Caution: A few people experience gastrointestinal upset when eating this fungus, especially when overeating it, although finding enough for a meal can be somewhat challenging.

Comments: Upon close inspection, the tips on the branches of this coral have distinct points like the pearls or points above the arches of a crown (see photo). I have seen this coral in Oregon, Ohio, Michigan, Indiana, and Washington State.

Recipe: Not a favorite of mine. A curiosity yes, but not something I gather and store.

For a first taste, sauté until tender. For the adventurous, prepare a batter (tempura, flour, or panko). Coat cleaned crown corals, then deep-fry in 375°F peanut oil. Drain, salt, pepper, and serve (with Tapatío close at hand, as needed).

9 LOBSTER MUSHROOMS

The lobster mushroom is a mold covering a mushroom, typically *Hypomyces lactifluorum* (the mold) covering (read, engulfing) gilled *Lactarius* or *Russula* mushrooms. The hosts are gilled mushrooms, and thus begins the section on gilled mushrooms.

Lobster mushroom, a mushroom parasitizing a mushroom

LOBSTER MUSHROOM
Hypocreaceae (*Hypomyces lactifluorum*, Schw. ex. Fr. L. Tul. & C. Tul.)

Origin: *Hypo* means "under" or "beneath," and *myces* means "mushroom." *Lactifluorum* refers to the *lactarius* (milky) mushrooms.

Season: July–Oct in Washington

Identification: This parasitic mold, a fungus attacking a mushroom, turns the host's flesh into a dense (and edible) mass covered with a bright reddish orange to reddish purple, thin, glasslike crust displaying pimple-like bumps. Typically *Russula brevipes* and *Lactarius piperatus* are parasitized. The lobster mushrooms often have a glossy, stained-glass–like appearance. The host mushroom is typically still visible in the fungal mass, although it may be grossly deformed. Mushroom is 2"–5" tall and up to 4" wide.

Spores: Spores are transparent, spindle shaped, and warted.

Habitat: Found in conifer and hardwood forests in conjunction with *Lactarius* and *Russula* mushrooms.

Look-alikes: No mold look-alikes, but mushroom host may vary. See "Caution" and "Comments."

Edible: Edible and choice with caution. Fresh is best.

Caution: It is standard practice in all mushroom field guides to warn against eating this mushroom. Sorry, but theoretically, it could parasitize a toxic host. No deaths or serious poisonings have been recorded as of this writing. Personally I have not had a bad experience. A safe, first time experience is to purchase this lobster mushroom at reputable Washington markets.

Store: Eat fresh.

Comments: With your first experience from the market, ask the purveyor where they found the mushroom. That will give you a place and purpose. In Washington search in forests and state parks along the coast.

RECIPE

Lobster Stew

1 lobster tail
4–6 lobster mushrooms chopped into ½" sections more or less
4 tbsp butter
4 tbsp olive oil
1 tbsp low-salt soy sauce
4 cups water
1 cup Riesling
1 lime
4 small red potatoes, quartered
2 stalks celery, chopped
2 shallots, chopped.
Salt and pepper
¼ tsp each thyme, oregano, and basil
1 cup sour cream
Sriracha on the side

Boil the lobster, the crustacean, for 2 minutes and save the boiling water. Boil the potatoes in the lobster water. Chop the boiled and cooled lobster into golf ball–size chunks. Place lobster chunks and potatoes in a pan with the chopped lobster mushrooms, shallots, and celery, then sauté over medium heat in half and half butter and olive oil. Right before browning occurs, squirt in a tablespoon-plus of Sriracha and the juice from ½ a lime. Add white wine, soy sauce, thyme, oregano, and basil. Serve as a soup appetizer with a dollop of sour cream. Prepare for 3 or 4 guests. Guests may salt and pepper as desired.

10   Gilled Mushrooms

Gills attached

Gills detached

Gills decurrent

Gills partially attached

Washington's edible gilled mushrooms are a challenge to identify, with severe consequences for mistakes. The following principles of identification help eliminate the dangerous species. Circumspect and positive identification are a must. If you are not certain of its identification, leave it alone.

General characteristics of gilled mushrooms include caps (pileus) that are nearly round, bell shaped, conical, convex, and vaselike. As these various caps mature, they may broaden and flatten. Gills may be attached or detached (see photos) in reference to the stem. And in many species, they may extend down the stem (decurrent). Attachments of gills may be partial or adnexed—that is, barely attached. Gills may be thick or thin, closely spaced (crowded), or broadly apart. Stems (stipes) are of various lengths, usually centered, but not always. Stems may be of equal thickness from cap to attachment, or vary in thickness in either direction. The bases of most *Amanitas* are bulbous or egg shaped, from which the fruiting body emerges. Stems, in general, may be brittle or rubbery, delicate or tough, smooth to the touch, or rough, hairy, powdery, dotted, or lined—even netted—they are either: solid, hollow, striated, or filled with soft pith. The stemless gilled mushrooms are typically attached to wood. When emerging, mushrooms may have a veil. The gill-protecting veils are either full, covering the entire emerging mushroom, or partial, simply protecting the gills. These veils rupture as the mushroom matures, leaving clues to its identification. Remnants of the ruptured veil may be left on the cap and the cap margins. On many species the remnant leaves a ring on the stem. Rings on the stem may be single or double, fixed to the stem, or move freely up and down like a wedding ring on the finger. These are several of the characteristics of gilled mushrooms that facilitate their identification.

Considering all the variables, it is safe to say your first experiences with gilled mushrooms should be with an expert. Join a mycology group and participate in field experiences identifying gilled mushrooms. In time you will discover a special few that you enjoy as food. For me the two easiest-to-identify gilled mushroom species are the shaggy mane, *Coprinus comatus,* and the oyster mushroom *Pleurotus species.*

Shaggy manes roadside in a campground

SHAGGY MANE, SHAGGY INK CAP, LAWYER'S WIG
Agaricaceae (*Coprinus comatus* [O. F. Müll.] Pers.)

Origin: *Coprinus* from Greek meaning "dung"; Latin *comatus* for "long-haired"

Season: Summer and fall

Identification: *Coprinus comatus* is fairly common in Washington. The young fruit bodies first appear as emerging white cylinders pushing up from the ground. They continue to grow, forming into an elongated, shaggy, bell-shaped cap covering most of the stem. The stem then continues to grow, the bell-shaped cap begins to open and disintegrate to a black ooze. Caps are white at first and covered with scales (shaggy). Scales are pale brown at apex, providing the origin of the name. Crowded free gills change rapidly (within hours) from white to pink, then to black, and then dissolve in what appears to be black ink. It is deliquescent; that is, it absorbs water and is best dry-brushed clean, not washed. The stem (stipe) has a loose ring and measures 3"–12" tall and 0.5"–1" in diameter. The flesh is white when young and fresh, and the taste is mild and unique.

Spores: Black. The spore print is black-brown.

Habitat: Shaggy manes grow in unexpected places—yards, grassy roadsides, hidden under shrubs, aprons of grass along wood lots, edges of dirt roads, and meadows throughout North America—often fruiting in large numbers. Look around campground edges. Gather young, fresh caps; available late summer through fall.

Look-alikes: A close relative is the alcohol inky, *Coprinus atramentarius*. The alcohol inky is also edible, but as the name suggests, not with alcohol. Mushroom chemistry (coprine) inhibits the liver enzyme, acetylaldehyde dehydrogenase, that detoxifies alcohol. Should you eat the alcohol inky, wait 2 days before imbibing.

Edible: The young mushrooms, before the gills start to turn black, are edible. Eat as soon as possible after collecting. Use liquid left from cooked shaggy manes with chicken stock or in balsamic reductions. This mushroom's robust flavor makes tasty dishes, from tetrazzini to cream soups. Eating the dissolving mushroom is not harmful, but the slimy mouthfeel and scant flavor are unrewarding. Washing in water hastens their deterioration. This fragile mushroom requires careful collecting and gentle handling.

Medicinal: *Coprinus comatus* polysaccharides assist recovery in liver-damaged rats and may have human application, but there have been no human trials (Aina et al., 2014).

Caution: Let these mushrooms emerge from the ground before harvesting to be certain they are not toxic *Amanitas*. As mentioned, a few *Coprinus* species contain coprine, a myco-toxin. Do not consume these mushrooms before, after, or while drinking alcohol. Be certain you have *Coprinus comatus* before consuming, the safer mushroom to eat. A few individuals have allergic reactions after eating shaggy manes—unfortunately, you won't know until you try it—and in most cases, it is simply delicious. *Coprinus* species accumulate heavy metals including mercury, so avoid mushrooms growing in or around contaminated sites.

Storage: For eating and storage, process (sauté) immediately or within 4 hours after harvest to avoid undesirable changes to the mushroom. For long-term storage, microwave, sauté, or simmer until limp, double-bag, and store in a refrigerator for several days or freeze.

Comments: I eat only this species of *Coprinus* and find *C. comatus* while driving down a highway or biking backcountry roads. It can even pierce through cracks in asphalt. Use the dark juice of the spoiling mushroom as ink, as a hair coloring, as face and body paint, as a fly repellent, and as a dye for fabric, paper, and wool. The species is cultivated in China as food. Vietnamese purveyors place shaggy manes upside down inside egg cartons to prevent deterioration during transport, affording an extra day or two before the black disintegration.

RECIPE

Shaggy and Simple

8 shaggy mushrooms, uncut
6 tbsp olive oil, divided
2 tbsp (or more) butter
¼ cup diced sweet onion
¼ pound linguine noodles

I love shaggy manes simply prepared: Sauté the whole mushrooms in half butter, half olive oil and optional diced onions. The dark juices that emanate during cooking should be poured off and saved as a soup flavoring. Draining also hastens the cooking process. Next add mushrooms and onions to room-temperature olive oil, sprinkle on dry or fresh oregano and basil, and add about 10 fennel seeds. Heat the remaining oil and mushrooms gently, while preparing linguine noodles. Toss the noodles with the mushroom oil sauce, sprinkle over with fresh Parmesan, and serve.

The **PLEUROTACEAE** family harbors several of the best edible and medicinal mushrooms available in the wild, or over the counter, and you can grow your own (see appendix B, "Grow Your Own"). Oyster mushrooms are widely available in Washington during the late spring and throughout the summer and fall.

Oyster mushroom gills

OYSTER MUSHROOMS
Pleurotaceae (*Pleurotus populinus*, Hilber & Mill.); *Pleurotus pulmonarius* (Fr. Quel.)

Origin: Latin *pleurotus* means "sideways" or "side ear."

Season: Early summer into winter.

Identification: There are as many as 11 species of oysters, all saprophytic, white rot fungi, typically growing in colonies on wood (often on dead alder, poplar, aspen, and, more rarely, conifers in Washington). Gills are attached running down the stem (decurrent). Stem (stipe) is short and off to the side, supporting a flat or funnel-like cap. Short stem may be absent. *P. pulmonarius* (3"–5" wide) is cream-colored to tan, with lilac-hued spore print, and found on dead and living deciduous trees and conifers. *P. populinis* (2"–5" wide) is typically lighter in color, white to off-white, and found on cottonwoods, aspen, and alder. Take your time and be thorough when identifying, cross-reference in several books, and hike with an expert.

Pleurotus populinus

Spores: White to gray, whitish spore print

Habitat: Find *P. populinus* and *P. pulmonarius* on alder, maple, birch, aspen, and conifers. They grow in dense clusters and with as many as a half bushel on a large downed tree. The same tree may support mushrooms for 3–4 years, until lignin decomposition is complete.

Pleurotus pulmonarius

Look-alikes: *Pleurocybella porrigens* (common name angel wings), long considered an edible mushroom, caused illness and death in Japan in the fall of 2004. It was a bumper crop, and those who ate the mushroom, infirm individuals compromised by weak kidneys, presented symptoms 13 to 18 days after consumption. Symptoms included weakness of extremities, tremor, consciousness disturbances, high fever, and seizures (caused by brain lesions). In acute cases, several days after onset of seizures, death occurred (see www.namyco.org/pleurocybella_toxin.php. Speculation suggests that binge eating of the mushroom and the large accumulation of a toxin in health-compromised victims was the cause. All the same I eat the *Pleurotus species* instead. There are plenty of edible oyster mushrooms to go around. *Porrigens* is smaller, whiter, almost translucent, and does not have a stipe.

Edibility: Excellent flavor! Pan-fry battered in panko (Japanese bread crumbs). Tastes great unbreaded too, with your favorite red or white seafood cocktail sauce. Sauté and add to pizza, stuff in eggs, improve sauces, simmer reductions, and make unique and delicious Chinese and Mexican dishes.

Medicinal: Preliminary research suggests that proteins from *Pleurotus* species may help lower blood pressure, acting as low-potency ACE inhibitors (Ching and Abdulla, 2011). Oyster mushrooms are antibiotic, antiviral, anticancer, anti-inflammatory, and may lower cholesterol. A heat labile lectin from *Pleurotus* exerted potent antitumor activity in mice bearing sarcoma S-180 and hepatoma H-22. Lectin treatment prolonged survival (Wang, Gao, and Ng, 2000). Pleuran, a polysaccharide isolated from *Pleurotus ostreatus*, increased antioxidant activity in an animal model, reducing growth of colon lesions as compared to a control (Bobek, 2001). Another study showed that the ethanolic (the alcohol I use is Everclear) extract of the mushroom of *Pleurotus ostreatus* is rich in natural antioxidants

Pleurotus porrigens

(Jayakumar, 2009). Oysters may be the only food source of statins, a cholesterol-reducing chemical (Tobert, 2003; Memorial Sloan Kettering, 2013).

Storage: Oysters dry hard and crisp, intensi-fying their flavor and odor. Store in sealed canning jars. I prefer them fresh or cooked in a dish or sauce then frozen. Clean oysters with a brush and freeze without process-ing. Eat these fresh-frozen oysters within three months. Break off a frozen section and cook frozen to preserve flavor and texture.

Comments: Oysters are abundant in May and will be available through Dec. This table delicacy provides good nutrition and good medicine.

Panellus sp. oyster look-alikes but much smaller

RECIPES

One Simple, One Complex

Simple:

½ pound oyster mushrooms   Thick slice of smoked ham, chopped

Use equal amounts of olive oil and butter, or butter alone, and sauté until almost crisp. For the carefree, forget-about-my-health set, sauté in bacon fat, and when the ham begins to crisp, the mushrooms are done.

Complex:

Hey, these are oyster mushrooms, so here's a recipe I adapted from Jules Alciatore's original dish at the world-famous Antoine's Restaurant in New Orleans.

1 dozen 3"-wide (plus or minus) oyster mushroom caps	1 tbsp Pernod
	½ cup evaporated milk
2 finely minced shallots	½ cup Parmesan
2 tbsp butter	6 ounces finely chopped spinach
2 tbsp extra-virgin olive oil	2 tbsp bread crumbs
½ tsp anise seed, powdered	Sliced lime
2 tbsp cake flour	4 tbsp chopped parsley
1 tbsp sweet vermouth	Cajun salt

In a 12-inch frying pan over medium heat, melt a tablespoon of the butter and add the olive oil. Once the oil has come up to temperature, sear the mushroom caps until lightly browned on both sides. This should take about 2 minutes per side. Remove mushrooms from the pan and set aside on a separate plate. Season them with salt and pepper to taste. Into the same pan with the remaining oil and butter, add the shallots and anise seed. Cook for a few minutes until the shallots have softened. Add the Pernod and vermouth to the pan. Once the alcohol has evaporated, remove the shallot and set aside in a separate bowl. Melt the remaining tablespoon of butter in the pan. Add the flour and whisk until fragrant. This should take about 2 minutes. Whisk in the milk, making sure there are no lumps. Once the mixture starts to thicken, add the spinach and the shallot mixture. Check for seasoning. Add salt and pepper to taste. Now mix the Parmesan and bread crumbs together in a separate bowl. Turn your oven on medium broil. You are now ready to assemble the dish. Gather 12 ceramic soup spoons. Into each place 1 tablespoon of the spinach mixture, one large oyster mushroom cap, a tablespoon of the Parmesan mixture, and a drizzle of olive oil. Broil for 4 minutes or until browned. Keep warm in a low oven until ready to serve. Serve with lime slices and chopped parsley.

Coprinellus micaceous

MICA CAP, GLISTENING SHINY CAP
Psathyrellaceae (*Coprinellus micaceus* [Bull.: FR.] Vilgalys, Hopple & Jacq. Johnson)

Origin: *Coprinellus*, like *coprinus*, refers to living on dung. *Micaceous* means "mica like."
Identification: A secondary saprophyte feeding on vascular tissue after primary sapro-phytes break down the tougher parts of the wood. In other words, it is a couple steps down the fungal decomposition chain. The mushroom at first has a small oval cap, 0.5"–1.3", that becomes bell shaped and may have a dorsal bump or nipple (umbo). At maturity the cap flattens to convex, and the margin turns upward. Cap color is tan to yellow-brown to pale yellow and darkens at the margin as it ages. Color of the mushroom changes relative to hydration. Cap is grooved almost to apex; grooves mark position of gills underneath. Mica-like particles are on the cap, especially when young, and often wash off or fall off a mush-room as it matures (see close-up photo). The mica particles are definitive. You may need a hand lens, a useful tool for a mycologist. Gills are close, adnexed—narrowly attached to the stipe. Cap splits along gill plane as it ages. The mushroom autodigests itself like *C. comatus*, changing to a black oozing mass. Stipe is smooth, fragile, brittle, hollow, to 4" long and 0.2" wide. Stipe is white to dingy cream. Stipe may or may not have ring rudiment from veil. Flesh is white in stipe and darker in cap.
Spores: Brown or black spores

Habitat: Widespread, typically on decomposing wood and other organic matter that is aboveground or buried: gardens, disturbed ground, yards, edges of trails, vacant lots, roadsides.

Look-alikes: *Coprinus atramentarius* and *Coprinellus bisporus*, both edible species when not consumed with alcohol

Edibility: Edible, delicate flavor that can be overwhelmed. Do not overcook. Must be cooked, however, to deactivate compounds that may cause gastrointestinal stress. Best in sauces, egg dishes, and on toast points.

Mica on cap

Medicinal: *C. micaceous* has the highest potassium content in 36 mushrooms tested. Potassium is necessary for autonomic nerve function and supports a healthy heartbeat.

Comments: This species does not have coprine and may be eaten with alcohol. For a detailed description to complement this entry, go to: www://en.wikipedia.org/wiki/Coprinellus micaceus. They burst forth every spring from the same spot in my neighbor's backyard.

RECIPE

Sautéed Mica Caps

1 tbsp olive oil
1 tbsp butter
10–15 mica caps
Toasted sourdough points
Salt and pepper
Arugula
Mayonnaise

In a hot nonstick pan at medium heat, sauté the mushrooms, and then spread them on sourdough toast points, with a thin covering of mayo topped with arugula. And for certain, try a couple mushrooms on the hoof hot out of the skillet.

Honey mushrooms

HONEY MUSHROOMS
Physalacriaceae (*Armillaria ostoyae* [Romagnesi] Herink; *Armillaria nabsnona* Volk and Burdsall; *Armillaria mellea* [Vahl.] P. Karst)

Origin: *Armillaria* from the ring-shaped veil, and melle(a), meaning "honey colored"
Season: From early summer to early winter; may reappear at the same location in the same year and in consecutive years
Identification: With as many as 10 species and at least 4 in Washington, this variable and parasitic mushroom eventually destroys its host. The mushrooms are medium-size, caps range from ¾" to 8" in size, and color varies from light honey like to dark brown, slimy when wet, and most have a clearly visible cottony ring, yellow tinged (see photo). Stem (stipe) varies from 2" to 6" inches and is tough and fibrous, shredding to long fibers. Gills vary from off-white to dark brown. They are close and attached and may run slightly down the stem. Flesh is white with a strong, sweet odor. Cap almost always has a cluster of tiny scales at its center—shiny and sticky when wet—and often with tufts of tiny hairs with a thicker, darker concentration toward middle of cap. Found in large clumps (for safety's sake, do not harvest lone specimens). They release copious amounts of pale cream, smooth elliptical spores. Because of toxic look-alikes, always, *always* make a spore print. Once you are certain of the species, stay with that location and don't get creative—there are too many poisonous look-alikes. They will produce on the same dead or dying trees for several years.

Spore: Spore print pale cream to white

Habitat: These forest-damaging parasites attack both deciduous and coniferous forests, and are found on living or dead trees, stumps, roots. It is widely distributed in the East and in California, as well as the Pacific Northwest and Washington, where several varieties of the genus reside. In the Midwest and East, they attack beech and other hardwoods. In the West they grow on conifers, willow, and salmonberry. This is important: Once you have safely identified and tasted it, find it at the same spot the next year.

Look-alikes: Get to know *Galerina marginata* before eating honey mushrooms. This poisonous look-alike has rusty-brown spores, not white or creamy. Always make a spore print. Avoid *Omphalotus* species (jack-o'-lantern) and *Gymnopilus* species—orange spore prints.

Edible: One way to prepare the caps is by boiling them in slightly salted water for 2 minutes. Discard water then sauté in bacon fat or butter, put in sauces, and season with garlic and fresh basil.

Medicinal: *Armillaria spp.* are popular ingredients in traditional Chinese medicine for treating geriatric patients. A recent study indicated that growing the mushroom on maize (corn) provides a good substrate to maximize the potency of DPPH radical scavenging and anti-edema activities of *A. mellea*. Phenolic compounds (extracted with ethanol) are the antioxidant—not the level of polysaccharide content (Lai, 2013). Another study concluded that *A. mellea* extracts possess potent free-radical scavenging and anti-lipid peroxidation activities, especially aqueous extractions, in brain homogenate studies (homogenized brain tissue culture) (Ng et al. , 2007).

Storage: Eat cooked fresh or cook into recipes and store in freezer. Drying toughens the mushroom and it does not reconstitute easily.

Comments: These mushrooms require careful identification. Always look for the ring and scales and the darker fine scales that are thicker toward the center of the cap, and always pinch and tear the stipe, testing how it shreds and its toughness. A spore print is necessary. Understand, there is so much variability in the genus that identification must be circumspect; when all tests out, cook and taste just a little with much trepidation.

Honey mushrooms
spore prints

R. xerampilina is edible, but many *Russulas* are not.

RUSSULALES
Russulaceae (*Russula xerampelina* [Fries] SF Gray)

Origin: Latin *russus* means "red." *Xerampelina* means "dried vine leaves," thus the color of dried vine leaves.

Season: Summer and fall

Identification: General characteristics: Large forest group of widespread, somewhat brightly colored, and brittle-textured gilled mushrooms that break easily and cleanly into many pieces. Medium to large size typically, with caps of various colors: red, purple, yellow, green, and blue. Caps typically convex, flat, or centrally depressed, and diameter is about equal to length of the stem. Mushrooms lack veils, rings, and volvas. The crumbly brittle texture (as is true for *Lactarius*) is due to spherical cells that move past each other rather than long, entangled hyphae as in other mushrooms. Gills are brittle, attached, and run slightly down stem. This is a difficult genus to key down (especially in the field) to the species. Many are edible, most others are mildly toxic, and a few are toxic (see "Caution," below).

As for *R. xerampelina*, when handled, the odor is of boiled shrimp or crab, and scent gets stronger with age. The white stem may have pink tinges and stains yellow and then brown when broken, pinched, or rubbed. Gills are yellow. Cap is bright red to maroon or burgundy; center is darker than edge. Cap smooth, sticky when young; in old age edge may be lined.

Caution: Do not eat *Russulas* that bruise red, red to black, or directly to black. This includes *Russulas* that turn red or grayish when cut. These color changes may take time to show; be patient, and make a spore print. This will provide a modicum of protection from the most toxic *Russulas*. *Russula subnigricans* is implicated in the death of a Korean man. The species has tentatively been found in the southeastern United States.

Spores: Pale yellow to yellow spore print

Habitat: Forest terrestrial and mycorrhizal (symbiotic) partner with conifers and hardwoods. Found nationwide, and found in abundance in Washington.

Toxin: Sesquiterpenoids cause vomiting, gastrointestinal distress, and diarrhea. Vomiting usually ends the episode.

Edibility: *Many inedible. R. xerampelina is edible.*

Medicinal: A few *Russulas* have antitumor lectins.

Milklike exudate from *Lactarius* mushroom

LACTARIUS

Like other members of Russulaceae, *Lactarius* species have a crumbly, brittle texture. They typically may (or may not) exude a milky substance when pinched, torn, or cut, especially in younger specimens. The milklike exudate may be scant and difficult to find in a few species, especially older specimens. Color of the milk stains, when exposed to air, are often critical in identification. These colors may develop almost immediately or over an hour. Other identification characteristics in many members of the genus are concentric rings or zones of color on the cap. Typically the cap is about as wide as it is tall. Melzer's solution and KOH (potassium hydroxide) are chemical stains and tests that narrow identification. For more help in chemically identifying these species, see www.mushroom expert.com/lactarius.html.

Candy Cap
Saffron Milkcap

Candy caps HUGH SMITH

CANDY CAP
Russulaceae (*Lactarius rubidus*, Methven)

Origin: *Lactarius* means "milk" or "milky"; *rubidus* means, roughly, "red."
Season: Fall
Identification: A wrinkled, reddish brown to orangish, or cinnamon-brown cap, convex at first, then flat or slightly vase shaped. Cap size ¾"–3.6" wide, ¾"–3" tall (small to medium-size), exuding a white, scant, watery "milk." Dry, slightly bumpy cap. Gills are attached, decurrent (running down stem slightly), pink in color or pale orange, darkening with age. Stem is brittle, mostly even in width top to bottom, with, perhaps, orangish hair or fuzz near base. Taste is bitter when raw and sweetens with age. Flesh is nonstaining pale orange; gills with age show cinnamon-brown stains.
Spore: White to yellowish
Habitat: Found in the fall in conifer forests. Mycorrhizal with Douglas fir. Also found with live coastal oak and tan oak. South Coast Douglas fir forests for best results, later in the fall as you go south.
Look-alikes: Read "Caution," below.

Caution: It is possible to mistake candy caps with poisonous mushrooms. Picking the mushroom from the duff with fingers helps identify the brittle stem. Then break the mushroom in half and look for the thin, non-color-changing milk that exudes (sometimes) scantily from the gills and flesh. Typically, candy caps grow on the ground or emerge from duff or moss covering dead trees but not on the tree itself; this also helps in identification. The best help I can give you is a website that goes into tedious detail on candy cap identification. You do not want to eat a deadly *Galerina*. Go to www.mykoweb.com/articles/CandyCapComplex.html.

Edible: Candy caps are esteemed by mushroom gourmands. Prepare in savory dishes and experiment with sweet treats, even ice cream.

Storage: Dry in a food dryer and place in a sealed jar for later use.

Comments: This versatile mushroom goes well with and as an addition to wine and spirits. Its biggest drawback is difficulty in identification, especially first-time experiences (join a mycology group). Characteristics of color, odor, cap texture, and watery latex are helpful: Cap is not sticky, it is dry, flesh odor mild, and pleasant. A few foragers say maple-colored cap has texture that is bumpy like an orange skin, and cap skin is dull, not shiny or glossy.

RECIPE

Candy Cap Cookies

Candy caps are dried and added to champagne and wine. Add them in your crème brûlée recipe or make these Candy Cap Cookies.

½ tsp vanilla
2½ cups flour, sifted
1 cup dried or 2 cups fresh chopped candy cap mushrooms
1 cup butter, softened, plus extra for sauté
1 cup sugar
1 egg
½ cup toasted pecans, chopped

If mushrooms are dried, rehydrate and squeeze out water. Use fresh candy caps too.

Whether fresh or dried, sauté mushrooms in 2 tablespoons of butter. Then soften the 1 cup of butter, and blend in sugar, egg, and vanilla. Keep stirring while adding in flour, nuts, and candy caps.

Roll dough into logs (use sushi roller) or form into dollops, lay on wax paper, and freeze.

Preheat oven to 350°F. Cut cookie logs into ¼" slices and place on ungreased cookie sheet. Bake for 8–10 minutes until bottoms of cookies are golden brown. Dollops are removed to the greased cookie sheet without slicing.

L. deliciosus HUGH SMITH

SAFFRON MILKCAP, ORANGE-LATEX MILKY
Russulaceae (*Lactarius deliciosus* [Fries] S.F.G.)

Origin: *Lactarius*, from Latin, means "milk" or "milky." *Deliciosus* is Latin for "delicious."
Season: Fall: Aug into Nov
Identification: *Lactarius deliciosus* is mycorrhizal partner with conifers. It is a medium-size gilled mushroom (cap is 2"–5½" wide) with a carrot-orange cap that when young stains red and then stains green with age. Cap is smooth with distinct bands (shades of color). When mature the mushroom cap is convex or vase shaped with a depressed (sunken) center. Margin is inrolled, and the entire mushroom may become vase shaped with age. Slimy or viscid when wet, it exudes an orange "milk." Flesh is yellowish cream or orangish fading to orange-yellow and finally greenish. Gills are crowded, decurrent (attached and running down the stem). Gills yellow or pale orange and may exude an orangish juice when cut with knife. No veil and no ring (annulus). Stalk is same color as cap, somewhat short: 1¼"–2¾" long, ⅝"–1" thick, brittle, orangish, and bruises to green as it ages, not sticky. Flesh is pale yellow to orangish, and orange exudate displays when cut. Taste is mild to bitter.

Spore: Bright cream (buff) spore print.

Habitat: Pine forests, and in pine and cedar bogs with other conifers. Often found in pine plantations.

Look-alikes: *L. rubrilacteus* is banded and similar, releases dark-red- to purple-colored milk, and has defined orange and red-brown rings, whereas *L. deliciosus*'s rings are less pronounced and the latex color is orange. Another look-alike, *L. thyinos* is found in wetland cedar bogs in the East and has a sticky stalk. Green-staining characteristic of *L. deliciosus* is indicative.

Edible: Good find. Slow-cook or grill while basting with oil. Add to casseroles.

Medicinal: Weakly antibiotic chemistry has been tested, and they are weakly mutagenic (Rogers, 2011, p. 249).

Comments: *Lactarius* species exude from the gills and flesh red, orange, blue, and white "milk." That fact puts you halfway home. They are crumbly mushrooms, typically breaking into bits as you squeeze them in your hand. The mushrooms with orange or red milk are usually edible when slow-cooked, but change water twice for first experiences.

RECIPE

Pickled Milk Caps

Pickle these mushrooms in vinegar—I suggest a ready-prepared pickling spice mix.

1–2 pounds whole or halved mushrooms
Pickling spices
Pint white vinegar
1 tsp ground ginger root
2 tsp olive oil
2 tsp salt
2 cups water

Add about a teaspoon of fresh-ground ginger to the pickling spices, tie off in a bag, and immerse in a blend of 2 cups water, 2⅓ cups white vinegar, 2 teaspoons olive oil, and 2 teaspoons salt. Simmer herbs for 5 minutes, then add whole or halved mushrooms and cook for 15 minutes. Remove herbs and can in hot, sterilized jars. Store in refrigerator for up to 4 weeks.

TRICHOLOMATACEAE

According to Michael Kuo (www.mushroomexpert.com), members of Tricholo-mataceae are often identified by the process of elimination; that is, eliminate the dangerous mushrooms by a circumspect documentation of characteristics. In each case, make certain the spore print, shapes, and colors eliminate *Amanitas*, *Russulas*, *Lepiotas*, *Limacellas*, *Lactarius* (milk caps), and members of Hygropho-raceae (waxy caps). For more details see Kuo at www.mushroomexpert.com/tricholomataceae.html. Here are a few edibles that take circumspect identification.

Fried Chicken Mushroom
Matsutake
Wood Blewit

L. decastes HUGH SMITH

FRIED CHICKEN MUSHROOM
Tricholomataceae (*Lyophyllum decastes* [Fr. Ex. Fr.] Sing.)

Origin: *Lyophyllum* connotes "violet like" in Latin, and *decastes* is Latin for 10, and yes, these mushrooms are found in groups of 10.

Season: Late summer, fall, spring

Identification: Medium-size mushroom, 1"–5" cap growing in dense and large clusters on the ground. Cap is smooth. Cap color variable from whitish to light brown, to gray-brown, even yellowish brown, to tan. Color, in contrast to gills, does not change when cap is pinched. Cap feels slippery and smooth. Cap convex to almost flat with inrolled margin when young and then upturned margin as it ages (no veil, no ring). Gills are white (spores pure white) but may age to gray and may turn yellow to brown when bruised or pinched. Gills are in multiple tiers of longer and shorter gills. Gills are close, attached to or slightly descending stipe. Stipe is white with brown flushing towards base, and may be off-center or centered, 1"–3" long, ½"–¾" thick, smooth and tough, spongy to a squeeze. Stipe surface is moist, fibrous, and striated, may be powdery at apex, and possibly with scales and fibrils peeling down stalk. Mushroom is colonial in nature, often found in large, heaping clusters. For more details see: www.mushroomexpert.com/lyophyllum_decastes.html.

Spore: Round, smooth and white.

Habitat: Roadsides, disturbed ground, grassy lawns, and in forests, and near forest edges.

Look-alikes: There are several potentially toxic look-alikes: *Lyophyllum loricatum, L. connatum* (*Clitocybe connatum*), *Clitocybe dilatata,* and *Entaloma* species, so be cautious and detailed in your identification. (see "Caution" and "Comments").

Caution: More on look-alikes. *L. loricatum* color is variable: cap. *L. connatum* (*Clitocybe connatum*) cap is whitish, wavy, irregular. *Clitocybe dilatata* has pinkish to pinkish-brown cap edges downturned and slightly striated with center of cap slightly depressed; gills are darker, buff to pinkish buff. *C. dilatata* gills are close, decurrent to slightly adnate. *Entalomas* have a pink spore print and are found on soil. And *Lyophyllum decastes* should not be confused with the wood-inhabiting *Hypsizygus tessulatus* and *Gymnopus acervatus* (synonym *Collybia acervata*). *Gymnopus acervatus* are found heaped in tight colonies. They are smaller with reddish or pinkish tones to the cap and stalk. Gills are crowded and almost free. *Hypsizygus tessulatus,* a brown rot deciduous tree fungus (found on wood), has a tougher texture than *L. decastes,* but is similar. The honey mushroom, *Armillaria ostoyae,* is variable and fruits either on wood or in soil, but differs from *L. decastes* by having a ring around the stipe and large scales on the cap (although scales can wash off with age). *Clitocybe connate* (synonym *Clitocybe dilatata*) is also found along roadsides and in grasses but differs from *L. decastes* because of its white to buff cap and decurrent gills (not attached), producing ellipsoidal spores instead of round spores as found on *L. decastes. Pholiota terrestris* is smaller and has brown spores with a cap and stipe sporting large scales. The edible fairy ring mushroom, *Marasmius oreades,* also occurs in lawns and has white spores, but is distinguished by a reddish brown cap and fruits scattered to gregarious extensions or rings rather than in packed clusters.

Edible: With caution and detailed identification

Medicinal: The mushroom extracts from the dried mushroom or even deep-fried mushroom are antihypertensive in lab animals exhibiting ACE inhibition. They are also antitumor and hypolipidemic (fat-lowering) (Kokean, 2005).

Comments: Okay, so identifying mushrooms can be challenging and rewarding. *Lyophyllum decastes* is an example. This mushroom can be purchased online, and that is one of the best and safest ways to get familiar with it. In the field, remember it grows on the ground in tight clusters, has a white spore print, does not form fairy rings, does not have a ring around the stipe, and has attached gills that may run slightly down the stipe.

Mushroom Sauté

8–12 mushrooms
1 cup milk
2 eggs
1 tsp dry or 3 tsp fresh thyme
½ cup flour (rice flour)
½ cup bread crumbs

Keep it simple. Clean mushrooms with a brush. Slice in half lengthwise (or leave whole).

In a bowl whisk 1 cup of milk with 2 eggs. Salt. In a plastic bag mix ½ cup of flour with ½ cup of bread crumbs. Season with 1 teaspoon of thyme (dry) or 3 teaspoons fresh thyme. Set ½ cup of dry mixture aside.

Dredge mushrooms through egg mixture, then shake in bag to coat with flour-bread crumb mixture. Sprinkle a bit more over mushrooms from the ½ cup of reserved flour-bread crumb mixture. Fry in butter and olive oil, half and half of each fat, until crispy brown.

American matsutake rising from the duff

MATSUTAKE, PINE MUSHROOM
Tricholomataceae (*Tricholoma magnivelare*, Peck Redhead)

Origin: *Tricholoma* from the Greek, meaning "hair" and "fringe"; Latin *magnavela*, meaning "big veil"

Identification: Smooth, white, stocky, firm, gilled mushroom with thick stipe (stem) that tapers toward a point at the base without an amanita-like bulge. The edge of the cap curls under, and when young a tissue-like veil presents. Texture of cap and lower stipe is firm and often adorned with brown fibers or scales—stipe to 3" long. Cap matures to cinnamon-brown (2"–3" wide). Cottony ring present. Gills attached to the stem typically with a notch. Gills white at first and then cinnamon-stained. No color change when cut or sliced for use. Mushroom has a spicy odor.

Spore: Spore print is white.

Habitat: Scattered and gregarious under conifers, Douglas fir, lodgepole pines, ponderosa pine, sugar pine, noble fir, and Shasta red fir, specifically in western North America, Washington south through California and Mexico and north through British Columbia—also associated with rhododendron, salal, manzanita, madrone, and tan oak. Found in the autumn in the Pacific Northwest, Washington coast, and into the Cascades. Northeastern foragers locate the mushroom in jack pine forests; available Sept–Nov.

Look-alikes: *Amanita smithiana* has a slender stipe (that bulges slightly at the base) and lacks the spicy odor of the matsutake. Its flesh is softer and appears more slender and delicate rather than stout. *Tricholoma caligatum*, which is hairier, the hairs being darker brown fibrils, is not as stout or stocky as *T. magnivelare* and two *Catathelasma* species: *C. imperial* and *C. ventricosum*, which also have rings and pointed stipes but are darker colored, more gray than white, and lack the spicy odor, having what is called a farinaceous (starchy) odor of freshly ground grain or cucumber-like.

Edible: Eat matsutakes raw or cooked. They are in the same league as caviar and truffles. They improve all dishes and are especially delicious raw with salads or sautéed with a sirloin steak. Find traditional Japanese dishes featuring this coveted mushroom online at mssf.org/cookbook/matsutake.html.

Medicinal: Japanese use of matsutake goes back over 3,000 years. Clay statues, thousands of years old, of the fungus have been unearthed in Japan. One study indicated that the purified polysaccharide of *Tricholoma matsutake* is a potential source of natural broad-spectrum antimicrobial activity. They are antitumor and immunomodulating (Hou, 2013). Strong scientific evidence suggests eating matsutakes reduces or inhibits the growth of tumors and that they contain powerful free-radical scrubbers, preventing oxidative damage that may lead to cancer (Steady Health, 2010).

Comments: My first experience with matsutakes was in Japan, where I worked for the Department of Defense for three years, and then again in Washington where I bought a pound of fresh-picked matsutakes from a mushroom forager at a farmer's market. This is a safe first way to experience this mushroom and become familiar with its odor and other characteristics. This experience helps you avoid pitfalls in the bush. Like all gilled mushrooms, make your first experience in the wild with a knowledgeable guide.

Raw matsutake sliced on a salad

Blewit

WOOD BLEWIT
Tricholomataceae (*Clitocybe nuda* (Bull.) H. E. Bigelow & A. H. Sm.)

Origin: Latin *nuda* means "naked."

Season: Fall, early winter

Identification: These mushrooms are found singly and occasionally in arcs or fairy rings. Research suggests the genus *Lepista* is nested within *Clitocybe* and the genus *Clitocybe* is preferred, so . . . The convex cap (pileus) when young has a somewhat button shape with thin inrolled (rounded) edges. Cap is smooth, dry to moist, maturing to broadly convex with the edge typically turning wavy—cap size varies from 1" to 6". Color of cap and stem are variable: bluish-lavender color tends to fade toward tan or tinged with brown as they age. They maintain their original color better in shady locations. Aroma is fragrant. Gills are lavender, fading to tan or brown with age, and are crowded with a notched attachment to the stem. Stem (stipe) is thick with an enlarged base (slightly bulbous) up to 1" thick. Stem is 1"–3" long, ⅜"–1" thick, solid, dry, and scaly—pale purplish (violet gray, bluish lavender) or whitish when young, with darker striation (linear marks). Stem pales with age. As the mushroom matures, the stem may stretch out to several inches and fades from bluish or violet gray toward tan with a brownish tinge. Any attached mycelium has a slight bluish-lavender tint. Flesh is whitish-lavender. This is a difficult mushroom to positively identify. Blewits are harder to identify when older because of the tannish-brown color and stretched-out profile they develop (typical of so many mushrooms)—unless you are a knowledgeable and gifted forager, take your time, be circumspect, and avoid the old tan mushrooms. I pick the younger specimens, which conform true to blewit characteristics. All these shape and color changes require the forager to experience individual mushrooms in numerous stages. This is true for all mushrooms. Spore print of a blewit is a must.

Spores: Spores are whitish-buff with possibly a slightly pinkish tint. Print is pinkish-buff. Spore has an elliptical shape, is smooth, and appears colorless.

Habitat: Find *Clitocybe nuda* on grass or litter, pine duff, in the open, or in open woods and along trail edges. On cool nights before frost heralds an early autumn, the mushroom appears on piles of decomposing leaf and pine needle debris. Search around and under blackberry, alder, maple, oak, and other hardwoods in mature Washington woods, or in dumps of yard waste, and inside parks and cemeteries. Compost piles of grass and wood chips along edges of woods and lawns may be productive. Look in state park campgrounds and in shady, decaying leaf piles. In moderate climates, such as Washington coastal regions, the season may continue into Nov–Dec. I found *C. nuda* along the edge of mature white pine (5-needle) in thick needle duff.

Look-alikes: There are other mushrooms that are lavender or purple. *Cortinarius* species have a cobwebby veil. Avoid *Cortinarius* species! *Entolomas* (avoid) are likely to have thinner stems and a salmon/rouge-color spore print and are more gregarious. Other species may have brown spore prints and are more likely to occur earlier in the season. Be sure to make a spore print! When in doubt, throw it out(side)! (See "Caution," below).

Blewit spore print

Cobweb-like veil of inedible *Cortinarius* mushroom

Medicinal: Wood blewits contain the sugar trehalose, which is edible for most people but causes digestive disturbance in others. Blewit polysaccharides are hypoglycemic and may help regulate blood sugar. Various liquid extracts studied in vitro inhibited *Candida*, *E. coli*, *Staphylococcus aureus*, and *Streptococcus* species. Blewit extract (ethanol) showed antioxidant and antimicrobial properties and may be suitable in the food-processing industry (Mercan et al., 2006). Ethanolic and aqueous extracts of *C. nuda* inhibit cancer cell growth in vitro (Beattie et al., 2011).

Edible: These porous mushrooms waterlog on wet days. Many mycologists consider blewits tasty mushrooms with a somewhat delicate flavor. Prepare blewits in a cream sauce or sauté in butter. They are a good addition to stew, veal, pork, fish, poultry, cheese, rice, pasta, and pizza. Try them battered and deep-fried, or as more delicate tempura. Delicious as is, sautéed in butter. As mentioned, a difficult mushroom to be certain of; collect with an expert before trying it.

Caution: Spore prints of *Clitocybe nuda* vary as does the gill and cap color. Younger specimens display the typical characteristics and are therefore easier to identify. The spore prints of two poisonous look-alikes are different. *Cortinarius* has a rusty brown spore print and *Entolomas* have a dark-pinkish spore print. *Entolomas* do not show bluish-lavender gills, cap, and stipe as does *C. nuda* in its early stages of growth. *Entoloma nitidum* in Washington has a *dark* blue cap. Washington *Entolomas* are typically more slender-looking than *C. nuda*, and if there is a bulge at the end of the stipe, it is not as pronounced as *C. nuda*'s.

Both wood blewits may cause allergic reactions in sensitive individuals; this is more likely (but not exclusively) when the mushroom is eaten raw. In addition, blewits are difficult to identify, at least for me. Get precise and exact identification from an expert, then cook and taste a small amount, at your own risk.

Storage: Eat fresh or cook into dishes and refrigerate for 3 days or freeze for long-term storage.

Comments: Fly larvae may infest blewits. They do not store very well; use as soon as possible after picking. Wood blewits are used to dye fabric and paper green. One would think lilac or blue, but not so. Boil the chopped mushroom in water to release the color into paper or cloth.

RECIPE

Blewits and Thyme

One recipe found online a couple years ago fits nicely with my mushroom cooking philosophy: Let the mushrooms do the talking; that is keep it simple.

¼ pound of blewits
3 tbsp each of butter and olive oil
½ shallot, chopped
Fresh thyme

Sauté ¼ pound of blewits whole with 3 tablespoons each of butter and olive oil. Add to the pan ½ shallot chopped. Cook over medium heat until moisture disappears and mushrooms begin to brown. Sprinkle delicately with fresh thyme and serve.

M. oreades fairy ring

FAIRY RING MUSHROOM, MARASMIUS
Tricholomataceae (*Marasmius oreades* [Bolt. Ex Fr.] Fr.)

Origin: *Marasmius* is Greek for "drying out"; *oreades* is Middle English for "a mountain nymph."
Season: Summer and fall
Identification: Small- to medium-size mushroom, (1"–5" cap, smaller initially and then broadening (broadly bell shaped), found growing on lawns (grass) in groups, arcs, or fairy rings. Cap is whitish to pale tan to buff (light brown) with rolled-under margin that with age turns up as cap flattens. Central bump (umbo) always present. Gills are white, moderately spaced, notched, free to barely attached to stipe. Cap is hygrophanous, changing color as it dries, going from dark to a two-toned dark and light to light. Gills do not run down stipe (this is important) and are moderately broadly spaced. Stipe to 3" long, to ¼" wide, straight, whitish, rubbery and tough, minutely felted (finely hairy), and difficult to tear cleanly from the cap. Stipe may be smooth or have twisted ribs. There is considerable variability in color of this mushroom, depending on age and dryness or wetness: from yellowish brown and buff to white and gray to whole or part reddish brown.
Spores: Spore print white
Habitat: Broadly distributed in lawns, meadows, and grassy lots

Spore print of wet *M. oreades*. Note gill spacing and attachment or lack of attachment.

Look-alikes: There are three mushrooms that look similar, all of which are toxic. Be careful and circumspect when identifying this mushroom. *Clitocybe dealbata* and its cluster have similar characteristics but their gills are decurrent—that is, they run partly down stipe. *M. oreades* gills are free or slightly attached but do not run down the stipe. *Inocybe umbratica* looks similar to *M. oreades* but is stinky and has brown spores—make spore prints. And *Entalomas* look similar to *M. oreades* but have attached gills and dark-pinkish spore prints.

Edibility: Edible and good. Traditionally dried and used in soups, stews, and casseroles.

Medicinal: Test tube research used *M. oreades* extracts to cause apoptosis (cancer cell death) and showed potential in fighting triple negative breast cancer (Liao, 2017).

Comments: The penalty for making a mistake identifying this mushroom is severe. The *C. dealbata* toxin is muscarine as in *Amanitas*, often fatal.

MORE AGARICACEAE

The family Agaricaceae has numerous species of choice edibles and numerous toxic look-alikes. Tread carefully, my friend. Most species are stem and cap mushrooms, whereas others, like puffballs (covered earlier) and stinkhorns, have enclosed spore-producing bodies. This is a large family, and each member deserves strict and detailed identification. Be especially cautious with the next few mushrooms. Ideally, find them with an expert. Sign up for a field experience ASAP. These two mushrooms are worth the trouble.

Prince
Meadow Mushroom

Agaricus augustus HUGH SMITH

PRINCE
Agaricaceae (*Agaricus augustus* Fr.)

Origin: Latin *augustus* means "venerable."

Season: Summer, fall

Identification: Large, dry-capped gilled saprobe mushroom, 4"–9" wide, thick fleshed, firm, and white. It is dome-, square-, or hemispherical shaped in young stage, then expands to convex and eventually flat (flattened center) covered with concentric reddish-brown (golden-brown) scales over the whitish to yellowish cap. Pinching or bruising (rubbing) cap edge stains yellow and then turns reddish. KOH tests yellow. Gills are free (not attached to the stipe) and crowded, whitish at first with clinging tissue from veil, and then as they age they pass through a pinkish phase before turning dark brown (spore color) when mature. The young prince may be covered with white partial veil and dark warts covering the gills. The stipe is whitish to pale yellow, smooth, and adorned with a miniskirt-like ring. Stipe is thicker at base and narrows toward cap, to 9" tall and 1½" thick, with base of stem deep in substrate. Stipe fleshy (substantial) and may show shaggy golden-brown scales like on the cap. Stem scales are below ring, and typically stem is smooth (silky) above ring. Almond scent is indicative as is a non-yellow stem base.

Note: Sliced stem is not bright yellow inside or yellow at base. The mushroom does not grow out of a sack or egg. Stem may have a small-diameter, hollow center core. Taste not distinctive. Scent may be of almonds or anise, pleasant and mushroom-like.

Spores: Spore print chocolate brown. Individual spores elliptical, smooth, and purplish brown in color.

Habitat: Grows in woods on disturbed ground: edges of trails, and in urban areas: edges of coniferous forest, paths, gardens, lawns with rich humus

Look-alikes: Numerous look-alikes, several toxic: *Agaricus augustus*, the prince, when its skin is tested with 10% potassium hydroxide (KOH), it turns yellow. Dismiss all mushrooms growing from a sack or egg-like encasement (*Amanitas*). Eliminate any *Agaricus*-like mushroom that stains yellow when rubbing the cap or the base of the stem, or mushrooms that have a stem base that is yellow fleshed. Also dismiss species that when the base of the stem is crushed emit an unpleasant odor.

Tip: Potassium hydroxide solution can be purchased online. It is a caustic material, and dilution and handling should be done by an experienced person.

Edible: Choice, thick, and meaty with good flavor

Comments: See www.mushroomexpert.com/agaricus_augustus.html for excellent photos and more detailed information on chemical testing. *Agaricus bisporus* is the common over-the-counter mushroom available at groceries and is a good substitute for *A. augustus* when the latter is not available in the wild.

RECIPE

Prince Hoagie

2 large prince mushrooms
1 chopped shallot
Oil (your choice, enough to sauté the mushrooms).
Dill pickle
Tomato slices
Lettuce
A few arugula leaves
Hummus and mayonnaise

The prince, like portobellos (*Agaricus bisporus*), makes a great sandwich mushroom. Cook entire cap slowly with a whole chopped shallot, remove shallots before they blacken, then place mushroom and shallots, a dill pickle, a slice of tomato, lettuce, and arugula between the lips of a quality sandwich roll—think hoagie. Lather with hummus and/or mayonnaise.

A. campestris a worthwhile find—key it out carefully.

MEADOW MUSHROOM, PINK BOTTOM
Agaricaceae (*Agaricus campestris* L. Fr.)

Origin: *Agaric* means "tree fungus." *Campestris* means "growing in a field."
Season: Summer, early fall
Identification: White and squat mushroom (maturing to light brown), medium cap with pink lamella (gills) when young. Gills are free, narrow, and crowded, pink at first, aging to a chocolate or blackish-brown color. Cap is convex, maturing to nearly flat, smooth, or slightly scaly. Flat fibrous scales on cap, if present, are brownish. Cap is 1"–5" wide, with the stem (stipe) half as tall as the cap and to ¾" wide. Firm flesh is thick, white, and occasionally tinted light reddish brown to grayish brown. Cap edges may show pinkish if bruised but never yellow, orange, or red. Stem is equal more or less down its entire length, tapering toward foot. Foot is never yellow. Stipe is white and smooth above the small ring (annulus) and white and fibrous below. Stipe may turn pinkish if rubbed repeatedly or in wet weather. Ring on stipe, a remnant of partial veil, is thin and may not persist. Veil remnants may overhang edge of cap. Pleasing odor. Always dig up the base of one of these mushrooms when found in a group or fairy ring and make certain it is not growing from a bulb or sack like an *Amanita*.
Spores: Spore print blackish brown (chocolate); individual spores purplish brown, elliptical, and smooth surfaced

Habitat: Like the name suggests, found in open spaces typically: meadows, grassy areas, open fields, especially manure-laced pastures. I find them in the grassy trails through a restored meadow.

Look-alikes: Stipe of *A. campestris* does not change color to yellow, orange, or red when cut and bruised. This characteristic helps separate the meadow mushrooms from toxic look-alikes. Also, spore color, shape, and size is important in eliminating look-alikes. Look-alikes, to name a few, include *Amanita virosa*, *Lepiota naucina*, and *Agaricus hondensis*. *A. hondensis* is toxic but has a thick ring, bruises yellowish, and is a forest dweller. *A. xanthodermis* bruises yellow at the foot when sliced.

Edible: Delicious, firm, similar to commercial white button mushrooms in flavor and texture

Medicinal: Beta glucans in various agaric mushrooms have been tested in clinical trials and show immune modulation antitumor effects.

Comments: Mushrooms found in fields near mushroom-growing facilities are a close and edible look-alike: *Agaricus bisporus* is the common over-the-counter white mushroom available universally in markets. *A. bisporsus* spores escape the growing substrate and inoculate the surrounding fields. A manure-laden field helps this process.

Storage: Clean with a brush or with water, drain, and dry and then cook and freeze in dishes, or dry in food dryer. Young specimens will keep for 5 days in a breathable paper sack placed in a refrigerator.

RECIPE

Stuffed Mushrooms

8 meadow mushrooms
5 oz. Brie cheese
Oil: either butter or olive oil
¼ cup ground nuts, preferably hazelnuts

Cut stem from cap, leaving a hollow cap to receive nuts and cheese. Sauté mushroom caps in oil for 3 minutes over medium heat. Remove from heat and cool. Then place cheese in mushroom and sprinkle with finely chopped hazelnuts. Under a preheated broiler, broil stuffed mushrooms for 1–2 minutes or until the cheese bubbles brown. Serve warm.

11 Inedible, Toxic, and Hallucinogenic Mushrooms

Here is a small sample of inedible and toxic mushrooms of which I noted earlier. The list is far from complete and always will be—mycologists and amateurs are discovering new mushrooms every season. Please be cautious and circumspect in identification, get expert opinions, and stay safe. Find a few easy-to-find and easy-to-identify edible mushrooms and stay with them. There are so many dangerous mushrooms, too many to list in the limited space this book is given.

Amanitas
Clitocybes
Pholiotas
Cortinarius

Amanita muscaria in its many growth stages

AMANITAS
Amanita spp.

Family: Amanitaceae
Origin: *Amanita* is Greek for "mushroom."
Caution: Most *Amanitas* are inedible and toxic.
Season: Summer and fall
Identification: To identify *Amanitas*, dig out the base and underground part of the mushroom. In most cases (but not always) *Amanitas* arise from a volva—a capsule, sack, or swollen bulb. The shape of this base is important. If the mushroom emerges from a bulb-like swelling (volva) or sack, then reject the mushroom. This volva protects the developing mushroom and in its entirety looks somewhat egg-like. Slicing this volva vertically in half will reveal the immature mushroom and its gills—although the gills may be difficult to discern in early embryonic stage. The growing *Amanita* ruptures the veil protecting the gills, and remnants of the veil may remain on the cap and stipe. Rain may wash away these remnants. There may or may not be a ring (annulus). *Amanitas* come in a variety of colors: white, yellow, red, orange, green, and tan. But the volva (sack or egg) is indicative, and for species specificity, the spore shape, color, and size help complete the picture.
Spores: White spore prints across the genus.

Habitat: *Amanita* species are found nationwide and have affinities toward specific trees but aren't picky. Different species are often available for inspection Apr–Nov in Oregon. **Toxins:** The most potent toxins are α- and β-amanitin amatoxins. Psychoactive species contain psychoactive muscimol and the neurotoxin ibotenic acid that partially converts to muscimol after ingestion (Meuninck, 2014).

Edibility: *Most encountered are inedible and toxic.*

Comments: *Amanita* comprises over 600 species, many of which are toxic, a few psychoactive, and a few edible. *Amanita* poisonings account for about 95 percent of all mushroom consumption fatalities.

Amanita muscaria, psychoactive and toxic

Amanita virosa, one member of the destroying angel cluster

Toxic *Clitocybe* species with general characteristics

CLITOCYBES
Tricholomataceae (*Clitocybe* species)

Family: Tricholomataceae

Caution: Many inedible

Origin: Latin *clitocybe* means "sloping head" (funnel shaped).

Season: Summer–fall

Identification: A large genus (hundreds of species) of mushrooms, these medium- to large-size saprobes grow on the ground, on wood, and in open areas and forests. Caps are flat, broadly convex, or depressed in center, and generally smooth to the touch. Gills are fairly close, attached to the stem, and run down the stem or have a notched attachment (part of gill is attached, but notched below the attachment). Mushrooms are without veils, rings, or volvas. The smell may be sweet, but ingestion may be toxic.

Spores: Notched variety have pink spores. Spore print whitish to pale yellow or pale pink.

Habitat: Found nationwide in forests and in open areas. For more details, see Trudell, Ammirati, and Mello (2009) and Kuo (2007).

Toxin: Muscarine mimics the action of neural transmitter acetylcholine. Symptoms are blurred vision, sweating, salivation, abdominal cramping, diarrhea, tremors, convulsions, and constrictions of the pharynx. Five percent of the victims die.

Edibility: *Many inedible.* It may potentially contain deadly levels of toxic muscarine, and most are difficult to identify.

Pholiota aurivella, general characteristics of genus, colors vary

PHOLIOTAS
Pholiota spp.

Family: Strophariaceae
Caution: Many inedible
Origin: Greek derived from *pholos*, meaning "scale(s)" or "scaly."
Season: Summer and fall
Identification: These medium-size, fleshy mushrooms are white rot saprobes, and a few, perhaps, parasites. Many species have a distinctive scaly appearance on caps and stems. Although these species are beyond the range covered in this guide, here is a photo to begin your challenge. Most species require microscopic identification of spores and characteristics.
Spores: Light brown, brown, or yellowish brown
Habitat: Found nationwide on stumps and trees and, occasionally, on forest litter, typically in groups
Toxin: Amatoxins as in *Galerina* species destroy function of the liver and are often fatal.
Edibility: *Many inedible*. This group of fungi has both edible and poisonous members. Always forage with an expert and be absolutely certain before consuming.

Cobweb-like veil of the *Cortinarius* species

CORTINARIUS
Cortinarius spp.

Family: Cortinariaceae
Caution: Inedible
Origin: *Cortinarius* references the partial veil, from the root word "cortina."
Season: Autumn
Identification: Mycorrhizal with specific trees, these mushrooms have cobweb-like veil that covers the gills when young. Most specimens have close gills or slightly wider. Cap conical at first, then flatter. Stems with a swollen base.
Spores: Rusty brown to brownish red. Spore print rusty brown, whereas edible blewit has whitish-buff, pinkish-tinged print.
Habitat: Mycorrhizal with conifers
Edibility: *Inedible.*
Comments: Attractive mushroom—look but don't eat!

12 From the Market

Washington's farmer's markets carry a broad variety of wild and cultivated mushrooms. Most of the edible mushrooms in this field guide can be purchased at various times of the year at numerous farmer's markets. Also, edible and medicinal mushrooms are commonly available in supermarkets and Asian groceries. Chanterelles, lobster mushrooms, reishis, morels, oysters, and matsutakes are just a few of the wild types offered. Begin your foraging at the grocery for these wild types and you will become familiar with them—and that will make your outdoor foraging more productive.

Add the following mushrooms to your diet for great taste and improved health.

Chaga and maitake mushrooms are rarely, if ever, found in Washington, although a couple of sources tout finding them. They can be found online. Portobellos, enokitake, and shiitake mushrooms are cultivated in Washington State and are widely available.

> Truffles
> Chaga
> Maitake
> Portobello
> Enokitake
> Shiitake

Truffles from Washington State

TRUFFLES
Pizizales (*Tuber oregonense* and *Tuber gibbosum*)

Edibility: Edible, aromatic, versatile
Medicinal: Truffles chemistry is anticancer and has beneficial cardiovascular effect, provides an energy boost, and reduces blood lipids (fats), and they are sedative and may be helpful in pre-menopause relief and prostrate disorders. They help absorb calcium, may prevent diarrhea, and may fight eye cataracts of senility. These studies have been with truffles in Europe, the Middle East, and Asia. Research on Oregon and Washington truffles is ongoing.
Comments: Pigs and dogs are used to sniff out truffles in Europe. In Washington State you can get help training your dog to find truffles at https://truffledogcompany.com.

Chaga found on a white birch

CHAGA, CLINKER POLYPORE—MEDICINAL
Hymenochaetaceae (*Inonotus obliquus* Pers. FR.)

Edibility: Inedibile. Available online, used as a health-protecting tea or tincture.

Medicinal: The chaga preparation Befungin, available online as an alcohol extract, has been sold in Russia as a cancer treatment since the 1960s. In Siberia chaga extract and tea have been used for hundreds of years to treat stomach diseases, liver problems, worms, and tuberculosis. Cree called the mushroom *wiskakeeak omikih*—"the scab thrown against a tree to benefit mankind"—using it in smudging ceremonies and to keep tobacco burning in ritual pipe smoking. In a cell-culture study, chaga elicited anticancer effects on human lung carcinoma and colon adenocarcinoma—effects attributed to decreased tumor cell proliferation, motility, and morphological changes. Of note, the preparation produced no or very low toxicity in tested normal cells. Animal studies showed treatment with *I. obliquus* led to a significant decrease in blood glucose levels in induced diabetic mice (Lu, 2010).

Storage: Dried as a powder and sealed, it will keep for 6 months in a freezer.

Comments: Use a hatchet, cleaver, hammer, or axe to remove the fungus from the tree; it is most easily removed when frozen. Then chop the mushroom into small pieces for drying and subsequent use. Dry twice in an electric dryer or an oven at 125°F: First dry for 24 hours, and then remove and cool for 24 hours; dry again for another 24 hours or until bone dry. For finer tea powder, grind it in a heavy-duty blender, or for a smaller measure, use a cheese grater.

Recipe: Because of possible interaction with medications, use chaga extracts under your holistic health-care practitioner's supervision—good advice for using any mushroom in this book.

Maitake and Jill

MAITAKE, HEN OF THE WOODS, KING OF MUSHROOMS, DANCING MUSHROOM, CLOUD MUSHROOM
Meripilaceae (*Grifola frondosa* (Dicks) Gray.)

Edibility: A choice edible, gather when young. It may require diligent cleaning of the many cracks and crevices containing dirt and an occasional creature. Cooking softens its tough texture, and it goes well in all mushroom dishes—especially stews. Simmer slowly in salted water until tender.

Medicinal: Used traditionally to treat diabetes and hypertension. For thousands of years, Asians have included maitake as tonics in soups, teas, prepared foods, and herbal formulas to promote health and long life. Maitake extract is combined with radiation and chemotherapy in the treatment of cancer. The mushroom provides support for the immune system and improves blood pressure, blood sugar, and cholesterol levels. The mushroom is commercially available and marketed to "enhance immune function" and to treat HIV. Preliminary data suggests maitake may be useful in inducing ovulation in patients with polycystic ovary syndrome (PCOS). Laboratory studies show maitake can reduce the growth of cancer in animals. Maitake does not kill cancer cells directly but works through the immune system (organizing the body's defense system against infection). The studies test whether maitake improves the neutrophil count and function in patients with bone marrow disease. The neutrophils are white blood cells that help to fight infection—a Phase II Trial (Yukiguni, 2014).

Comments: Called *maitake* in Japan, the name means "dancing mushroom," perhaps because people dance for joy when they find it—available in international groceries and cultivated in the United States.

Agaricus bisporus, the white button, cremini, and portobello

PORTOBELLO, BABY PORTS, CREMINI, BUTTONS
Agaricaceae (*Agaricus bisporus* [Lange] Imbach)

Identification: This is the common over-the-counter mushroom sold in groceries across the country.

Medicinal: A controlled study of 2,018 women who ate *A. bisporus* had 64 percent fewer incidences of breast cancer than the control group. And by combining green tea with the mushrooms, the reduced risk skyrocketed to 90 percent—eat your portobellos, drink your tea.

Enokitake (Enoki)

ENOKITAKE
Physalacriaceae (*Flammulina velutipes* [Curtis] Singer)

Edible: Edible raw or cooked

Medicinal: Enokitake mushrooms are antiviral and antibacterial and contain the water-soluble antioxidant ergothioneine. The mushroom also contains flammutoxin, a cytolytic and cardiotoxic protein that appears to be nontoxic when absorbed orally (Lin and Shi, 1975). The Enokitake mushroom contains certain compounds that inhibit the formation of melanin due to the catalytic oxidation of polyphenol oxidase, as well as mushroom tyrosinase activity (Jang et al., 2003). *Flammulina velutipes* expresses the gene used to synthesize baccatin III, a paclitaxel precursor, thereby finding another mechanism for manufacturing paclitaxel, an anticancer, mitotic inhibitor (keeps cells from dividing).

Comments: Enokitake is a regular part of the Meuninck mushroom diet that also includes shiitakes, chicken mushrooms, hens of the woods, blewits, chanterelles, oyster mushrooms, honey mushrooms, puffballs of all kinds, morels, wood ears, aborted *Entalomas*, lion's manes, and an occasional dryad's saddle.

Shiitake grown on oak logs

SHIITAKE
Ganodermataceae (*Lentinus edodes* [Berk.] Pegler)

Edible: Versatile edible: savory dishes, Asian dishes, gravies, game, and beef

Medicine: Shiitake is one of the most studied mushrooms. In Japan, a glucan isolated from shiitake is a popular complementary and alternative medicine used in cancer treatment (Hyodo et al., 2005). Shiitake is used in Japanese Kampo medicine to alleviate arthritis, treat diabetes, lower cholesterol, and improve immunity. Prostate cancer research using shiitake extract, however, saw no improvement in human participants, although there was an increased number of days of survival in stomach cancer with no remission. Lentinan from shiitake is moderately antibacterial and selectively antifungal. Sulfuric-flavored compounds extracted from shiitake (*L. edodes*) showed inhibitory activity against platelet aggregation (clumping); the inhibitory activity is attributed to lenthionine, a sulfur compound, in shiitake essential oil (Shimada et al., 2004).

Caution: In perhaps less than 2 percent of the population, consumption of raw or slightly cooked shiitake mushrooms cause allergic reaction. Eliminate the effect, perhaps caused by the polysaccharide lentinan, with thorough cooking.

Storage: Purchase dried or fresh. Store in freezer either dried or fresh or cooked in a dish. Store dried mushroom with an airtight seal.

Comments: Look for dried shiitake that are light in color. It is my opinion that dried shiitake sourced from Japan looks better and tastes better than darker (looking a bit oxidized) shiitakes from China.

APPENDICES

A: Mushroom Recipes

http://foragerchef.com
www.wildmushroomrecipes.org/
http://theforagerpress.com/fieldguide/recipes/recipes.htm
www.mushrooms.ca/recipes/default
www.bonappetit.com/recipes/slideshow/mushroom-recipes-slideshow
http://indianhealthyrecipes.com/mushroom-recipes/
www.vegrecipesofindia.com/mushroom-recipes/
www.food.com/topic/mushrooms
https://livejapan.com/en/in-tokyo_train_station/article-a0001381/
www.tofugu.com/japan/japanese-mushrooms/

B: Grow Your Own

Many farmer's markets have mushroom-growing kits—a bag or other container filled with a substrate (wood chips or the like) inoculated with mycelia. This is a highly successful method to start with, and the mycelia can be reused.

Experiment. Try making spore prints from oyster mushrooms (oyster mushrooms are one of the easiest to grow) by scraping the spores from the spore prints with a razor blade until you have a teaspoonful, then incubate the spores in a container of distilled nutrient water. Here is the procedure: Add a quarter teaspoon of noniodized salt and one tablespoon of sugar or light molasses to a gallon of water, boil for 10 minutes to sterilize, and pour hot into a very clean and rinsed container made of glass, plastic, or stainless steel. Never use a container that held harsh chemicals or milk. Next, cover and cool the broth to room temperature, then add the teaspoon of oyster spores (wear a mask and avoid contact with spores). Cover the pot and incubate the spores in a shaded area between 60°F and 70°F. Shake the broth two or three times a day. If your spores are fresh and young, you may see thin threads of mycelia growing.

Use this spore-broth inoculation to pour over or mix into inoculate wood chips, cardboard, burlap, straw, and the like. And good luck.

There are many sources of mushroom kits online, search: home-mushroom -growing-kits.

C: Other Resources

www.mushroaming.com
Daniel Winkler provides field experiences and exotic trips to mushroom meccas in the northwestern United States, Tibet, and South and Central America. His website has numerous tips and tools to make your foraging experience more prolific.

www.natureswildharvest.com
Bill Cole and family offer mushrooms fresh and dried, as well as numerous other wild-crafted fruit, nuts, berries, and herbal teas.

www.Washingtonmushrooms.com
Offers grade A fresh and dried wild and cultivated mushrooms including morels, matsutake, porcini, chanterelle, black trumpet, dried shiitake, and portobello.

www.northernbushcraft.com
Provides excellent photos online of Pacific Northwest mushrooms. Be certain to visit this site.

www.mushroomexpert.com
This is Michael Kuo's excellent reference. Check out your find here before putting it in your mouth.

How to grow: "Gourmet and Medicinal Mushrooms," University of Kentucky, College of Agriculture Cooperative Extension Service, www.uky.edu/Ag/CCD/introsheets/gourmet.pdf

Growing mushrooms with coffee grounds: GrowVeg.com, www.growveg.com/growblogpost.aspx?id=261

Mushroom home-growing kits:
Mushroom Adventures: www.mushroomadventures.com
Fungi Perfecti: www.fungi.com

D: Recommended Books

Arora, David. *Mushrooms Demystified*. Berkeley, CA: Ten Speed Press, 1986. A large book, too heavy for the field, but filled with useful and entertaining material.

Kuo, Michael. *100 Edible Mushrooms*. Ann Arbor: University of Michigan Press, 2010. Winter reading from cover to cover; a great backup reference after leaving the field.

Lincoff, Gary. *National Audubon Society Field Guide to North American Mushrooms*. New York: Alfred A. Knopf, 1998. A field guide, yes. Take it with you, with Audubon's proven visual keys with generous coverage.

Meuninck, Jim. *Basic Illustrated Edible and Medicinal Mushrooms*. Guilford, CT: FalconGuides, 2015. Common mushrooms with incredible health value.

Meuninck, Jim. *Foraging Mushrooms Oregon*. Guilford, CT: FalconGuides, 2017. Edible and medicinal, another look at Northwest mushrooms.

Miller, Orson, and Hope Miller. *North American Mushrooms: A Field Guide to Edible and Inedible Fungi*. Guilford, CT: FalconGuides, 2006. If you can't find the mushroom in here, you may be on a different planet. A big, sit-in-front-of-the-fireplace guide to North American fungi.

Phillips, Roger. *Mushrooms and Other Fungi of North America*. Buffalo, NY: Firefly Books, 2010. Phillips does it right—another must-have guide.

Rogers, Robert. *The Fungal Pharmacy*. Berkeley, CA: North Atlantic Books, 2011. Impressive coverage—it should be in everyone's library. If you have a medicinal question about a mushroom, the answer is probably in this book.

Sept, Duane. *Common Mushrooms of the Northwest*. Calypso Publishing, Sechelt, BC, Canada. A good backup to *Foraging Mushrooms Washington*, a necessary second look.

Trudell, Steve, and Joe Ammirati. *Mushrooms of the Pacific Northwest*. Portland, OR: Timber Press Field Guide, 2009. If you live in the Northwest, you probably have this book. The visual key inside the cover is a great idea and very helpful.

E. Washington Mushroom Societies

www.psms.org/index.php
http://swmushrooms.org/resources__link
www.northwestmushroomers.org
http://cascademyco.org/resources-2/

BIBLIOGRAPHY

Aina, D. A., et al. "Antioxidant, Antimicrobial and Phytochemical Properties of Alcoholic Extracts of *Cantharellus cibarius*—a Nigerian Mushroom." *New York Science Journal* 5, no. 10 (2012): 114–120.

Bastyr University. "FDA Approves Bastyr Turkey Tail Trial for Cancer Patients." Article published November 30, 2012. bastyr.edu/news/general-news/2012/11/fda-approves-bastyr-turkey-tail-trial-cancer-patients.

Beattie, K. D., et al, "Ethanolic and Aqueous Extracts Derived from Australian Fungi Inhibit Cancer Cell Growth In Vitro." *Mycologia* 103, no. 3 (May–June 2011): 458–465.

Bernheimer, A. W., and J. D. Oppenheim. "Some Properties of Flammutoxin from the Edible Mushroom *Flammulina velutipes*." *Toxicon* 25, no. 11 (1987): 1145–52. See: www.ncbi.nlm.nih.gov/pubmed/3433291.

Bobek, P. "Effect of Pleuran (Beta-Glucan from *Pleurotus ostreatus*) on the Antioxidant Status of the Organism and on Dimethylhydrazine-Induced Precancerous Lesions in Rat Colon." *British Journal of Biomedical Science* 58, no. 3 (2001): 164–168.

Boucher, J. L., C. Moali, and J. P. Tenu. "Nitric Oxide Biosynthesis Nitric Oxide Synthase Inhibitors and Arginase Competition for L-arginine Utilization." *Cellular and Molecular Life Sciences* 55, no. 8–9 (1999): 1015–1928.

Bovi, M., et al. "Structure of a Lectin with Antitumoral Properties in King Bolete (*Boletus edulis*) Mushrooms." *Glycobiology* 21, no. 8 (2011): 1000–1009.

Chen, S., et al. "Aleuria Aurantia Lectin (AAL)-Reactive Immunoglobulin G Rapidly Appears in Sera of Animals following Antigen Exposure." *PLoS One* 7, no. 9 (2012). www.plosone.org/article/info%3Adoi%2F10.1371%2Fjournal.pone.0044422.

Ching, Lau Ching, Noorlidah Abdullah, and Adawiyah Suriza. Shuib Mushroom Research Centre, Institute of Biological Sciences, Faculty of Science, University of Malaya, 50603 Kuala Lumpur. International Conference on Mushroom Biology and Mushroom Products Section: Medicinal Properties 314 Characterization of Antihypertensive Peoptiles from *Pleurotus cystidiosus* O.K. Miller (Abalone Mushroom).

Cichewicz, R. H., and S. A. Kouzi. "Chemistry, Biological Activity, and Chemotherapeutic Potential of Betulinic Acid for the Prevention and Treatment of Cancer and HIV Infection." *Medical Research Reviews* 24, no. 1 (2003): 90–114.

Clark, D. A., and M. C. Adams. "A Commercial Nutraceutical Mix Metabolic Cell-Support (Mc-S) Inhibits Proliferation of Cancer Cell Lines In Vitro." *Australian Journal of Medical Herbalism* 21, no. 2 (2009): 39–42.

Cornell Mushroom Blog. "Eating the Chicken of the Woods." October 31, 2006. blog.mycology.cornell.edu/2006/10/31/eating-the-chicken-of-the-woods/.

Damte, Dereje, et al. "Anti-inflammatory Activity of Dichloromethane Extract of Auricularia auricula-judae in RAW264.7 Cells." *Toxicological Research* 27, no. 1 (2011): 11–14.

Dembitsky and others, 2013 Elsevier. Go to www.thefreelibrary.com/Bioactive+acetylenic+metabolites.-a0346931777.

Duncan, C. J., N. Pugh, D. S. Pasco, and S. A. Ross. "Isolation of a Galactomannan That Enhances Macrophage Activation from the Edible Fungus *Morchella esculenta*." *Journal of Agricultural and Food Chemistry* 50, no. 20 (2002): 5683–5685.

Ergonul, Pelin, Akata, et al. "Fatty Composition of Six Wild Edible Mushroom Species. *The Scientific World Journal*, 2013 Article ID 163964, 5 pages.

Fisher, M., and L. X. Yang. "Anticancer Effects and Mechanisms of Polysaccharide-K (PSK) Implications of Cancer Immunotherapy." *Anticancer Research* 22, no. 3 (2002): 1737–1754.

Hobbs, Christopher, Ph.D., L.Ac., A.H.G. (1998). "Medicinal Mushrooms III." Accessed February 23, 2014. christopherhobbs.com/library/articles-on-herbs-and-health/medicinal-mushrooms-3/.

Hou, Y., et al. "Anti-Microorganism, Anti-Tumor, and Immune Activities of a Novel Polysaccharide Isolate" from *Tricholoma matsutake*." *Pharmacognosy Magazine* 9, no. 35 (2013): 244–249.

Hwang, Chang. "Chlorinated Coumarins Form the Polypore *Fomitosis officinalis* and Their Activity against Mycobacterium Tuberculosis." *J. Natural Products*, 76, no. 10 (2013).

Hwang, Yun. "Hypoglycemic Effect Produced by Submerged Mycelial Culture of *Laetiporus Sulphureus* . . ." Biotechnology and Bioprocess Engineering, no. 15 (2010): 178–181.

Hyodo, I., et al. "Nationwide Survey on Complementary and Alternative Medicine in Cancer Patients in Japan." *Journal of Clinical Oncology* 23, no. 12 (2005): 2645–2654.

Jayakumar, T., et al. "In-vitro Antioxidant Activities of an Ethanolic Extract of the Oyster Mushroom, *Pleurotus ostreatus*." *Innovative Food Science & Emerging Technologies* 10, no. 2 (2009): 228–234.

Jang, Mi Soon, et al. "Inhibitory Effect of Enokitake Extract on Melanosis of Shrimp." *Fisheries Science* 69, no. 2 (2003): 378–384.

Jeong, S. C., et al. "Immunomodulation Activity from the Exopolymer of Submerged Mycelial Culture of *Phellinus pini*." *Journal of Microbiology and Biotechnology* 14, no. 1 (2004): 15–21.

Jeong, Yang, and Song Jeong. "*Ganoderma appalatum* a Promising Mushroom for Antitumor and Immunomodulation Activity." *Phytotherapy Pres.* 22, no. 5 (May 2008): 624.

Jimenez, E. Medina. (2008). A protein bound polysaccharide, PSK BMC Cancer, 8–78. See www.biomedcentral.com/1471-2407/8/78.

Jinjin Guo, et al. "Modulation of Lung Cancer Growth Arrest and Apoptosis by *Phellinus linteus*." *Molecular Carcinogenesis* 46, no. 2 (2007): 144–145.

Kerrigan, R. W. "*Agaricus subrufescens*, a Cultivated Edible and Medicinal Mushroom, and Its Synonyms." *Mycologia* 97, no. 1 (2005): 12–24.

Khan, M. A., et al. "*Hericium erinaceus*: An Edible Mushroom with Medicinal Values." *Journal of Complementary & Integrative Medicine* 10, no. 1 (2013): 1–6.

Kobayashi, H., K. Matsunaga, and Y. Oguchi. "Antimetastatic Effects of PSK (Krestin), a Protein-Bound Polysaccharide Obtained from Basidiomycetes: An Overview." *Cancer Epidemiology, Biomarkers & Prevention* 4, no. 3 (1995): 275–281.

Kodama, Somuta, and Nanba. "Effect of Maitake D Fraction on the Activation of NK Cells in Cancer Patients." *J. Med. Food* 6, no. 4 (Winter 2003): 371–377.

Kokean, Yasushii. "Effect of Frying with Edible Oil on Antihypertensive Properties of Hatakeshimeji (*Lyophyllum decastes*) *Food Sci. Technol. Res.* 11, no. 3 (2005): 339-343.

Kuo, Michael. (2014). "The Genus *Amanita*." MushroomExpert.com, June 2013. Accessed February 23, 2015. mushroomexpert.com/amanita.html.

Lai, M. N., and L. T. Ng. "Antioxidant and Antiedema Properties of Solid-State Cultured Honey Mushroom, *Armillaria mellea* (Higher Basidiomycetes), Extracts and Their Polysaccharide and Polyphenol Contents." *International Journal of Medicinal Mushrooms* 15, no. 1 (2013): 1–8.

Li, G., et al. "Protein-Bound Polysaccharide from *Phellinus linteus* Induces G2/M Phase Arrest and Apoptosis in SW480 Human Colon Cancer Cells." *Cancer Letters* 216, no. 2 (2004): 175–181.

Liao, C-S, S-Y Yuan, B-H Hung, and B-V Chang. "Removal of Organic Toxic Chemicals Using the Spent Mushroom compost of *Ganoderma* lucidum." *Journal of Environmental Monitoring* 14 (2012): 1983-88.

Lingling Fu, et al. "Effects of Ultrasonic Treatment on the Physicochemical Properties and DPPH Radical Scavenging Activity of Polysaccharides from Mushroom *Inonotus obliquus*." *Journal of Food Science* 75, no. 4 (2010): C322–C327.

Lovy, Alenka, Barbara Knowles, Ronald Labbe, and Linda Nolan. "Activity of Edible Mushrooms Against the Growth of Human T4 Leukemic Cancer Cells, HeLa Cervical Cancer Cells, and *Plasmodium falciparum.*" *Journal of Herbs, Spices & Medicinal Plants* 6, no. 4 (2000): 49–57.

Lu, Xueming, et al. "Phytochemical Characteristics and Hypoglycaemic Activity of Fraction from Mushroom *Inonotus obliquus.*" *Journal of the Science of Food and Agriculture* 90, no. 2 (2010): 276–280.

Lull, Christina, Harry J. Wichers, and Huub F. J. Savelkoul. "Antiinflammatory and Immunomodulating Properties of Fungal Metabolites." *Mediators of Inflammation* 2 (June 9, 2005): 63–80.

Luo, Y., et al. "Antioxidant Activities and Inhibitory Effects of *Auricularia Auricular* and Its Functional Formula Diet Against Vascular Smooth Muscle Cell In Vitro." *Food and Nutrition Sciences* 2, no. 4 (2011): 265–271.

Medical Mushrooms. "*Hericium erinaceus*, Lion's Mane Mushroom, Yamabushitake." Accessed February 23, 2015. medicalmushrooms.net/hericium-erinaceus/.

Memorial Sloan Kettering Cancer Center. "Lentinan." Last updated February 27, 2013. mskcc.org/cancer-care/herb/lentinan.

Memorial Sloan Kettering Cancer Center. "Maitake." Last updated October 28, 2014. mskcc.org/cancer-care/herb/maitake.

Mercan, Nazime, et al. "Antioxidant and Antimicrobial Properties of Ethanolic Extract from *Lepista nuda* (Bull.) Cooke." *Annals of Microbiology* 56, no. 4 (2006): 339–344.

Meuninck, Jim. *Basic Illustrated Poisonous and Psychoactive Plants.* Guilford, CT: FalconGuides, 2014.

Meuninck, Jim. (2013). Native American Medicine DVD. Meuninck's Media Methods, Inc.

Millard, J. T., et al. "DNA Interstrand Cross-Linking by Mycotoxic Diepoxide." *Biochimie* 86, no. 6 (2004): 419–423.

Mukai, H., T. Watanabe, M. Ando, and N. Katsumata. "An Alternative Medicine, *Agaricus blazei*, May Have Induced Severe Hepatic Dysfunction in Cancer Patients." *Japanese Journal of Clinical Oncology* 36, no. 12 (2006): 808–810.

Nakazato, H., et al. "Efficacy of Immunochemotherapy as Adjuvant Treatment after Curative Resection of Gastric Cancer. Study Group of Immunochemotherapy with PSK for Gastric Cancer." *Lancet* 343, no. 8906 (1994): 1122–1126.

Ng, L. T., S. J. Wu, J. Y. Tsai, and M. N. Lai. "Antioxidant Activities of Cultured *Armillariella mellea.*" *Prikladnaia Biokhimiia i Mikrobiologiia* 43, no. 4 (2007): 495–500.

Ng, T. B. "A Review of Research on the Protein-Bound Polysaccharide (Polysaccharopeptide, PSP) from the Mushroom *Coriolus versicolor* (Basidiomycetes: Polyporaceae)." *General Pharmacology* 30, no. 1 (1998): 1–4.

Nitha, B., C. R. Meera, and K. K. Janardhanan. "Anti-inflammatory and Antitumour Activities of Cultured Mycelium of Morel Mushroom, *Morchella esculenta.*" *Current Science* 92, no. 2 (2007): 235–239.

Noorlidah, Abdullah, et al. Evaluation of Selected Culinary-Medicinal Mushrooms for Antioxidant and ACE Inhibitory Activities. Evidence-Based Complementary and Alternative Medicine Volume 2012 (2012), Article ID 464238. http://dx.doi.org/10.1155/2012/464238.

Oluba et. al. "Modulatory Effect of Crude Aqueous Extract of Lingzhi or Reishi . . . on Hematological and Antioxicant Indices in *Plasmodium berghei*-Infected Mice." *Inter. Journal Medicinal Mushrooms* 16, no. 5 (2014): 499–506.

Peintner, U. et al. "The Iceman's Fungi." *Mycological Research* 102 (1998): 1153–1162.

PML Survivors & Supporters. "Is *Fomes fomentarius* a Miracle of Nature?" Go to https://groups.yahoo.com/neo/groups/PMLSurvivors/conversations/topics/578.

Powell, Martin. "*Auricularia auricula / Auricularia polytricha.*" *Mushroom Nutrition*. Accessed February 23, 2015. mushroomnutrition.com/auricularia-auricula.

Restrepo, A., et al. "Ulceration of the Palate Caused by a Basidiomycete *Schizophyllum commune.*" *Sabouraudia* 11, no. 3 (1973): 201–204.

Rihs, J. D., A. A. Padhye, and C. B.Good. "Brain Abscess Caused by *Schizophyllum commune*: An Emerging Basidiomycete Pathogen." *Journal of Clinical Microbiology* 34, no. 7 (1996): 1628–1632.

Robbins, W. J., et al. "A Survey of Some Wood-Destroying and Other Fungi for Antibacterial Activity." *Bulletin of the Torrey Botanical Club* 72, no. 2 (1945): 165–190.

Rogers, Robert. *The Fungal Pharmacy: The Complete Guide to Medicinal Mushrooms and Lichens of North America.* Berkeley, CA: North Atlantic Books, 2011.

Romano, P. R., et al. "Development of Recombinant *Aleuria aurantia* Lectins with Altered Binding Specificities to Fucosylated Glycans." *Biochemical and Biophysical Research Communications* 414, no. 1 (2011): 84–89.

Roth-Walter, F., et al. "M Cell Targeting with *Aleuria aurantia* Lectin as a Novel Approach for Oral Allergen Immunotherapy." *Journal of Allergy and Clinical Immunology* 114, no. 6 (2004): 1362–1868.

Saar, Maret. "Ethnomycology Data from Siberia and Northeast Asia on the Effect of *Amanita muscari*." *Journal of Ethnopharmacology* 31 (1991): 157–173.

Saviuc, Philippe, Patrick Harry, Corine Pulce, Robert Garnier, and Amandine Cochet. "Can Morels (*Morchella* sp.) Induce a Toxic Neurological Syndrome?" 48, no. 4 (May 2010): 365-72.

Shimada, S., K. Komamura, H. Kumagai, and H. Sukurai. "Inhibitory Activity of Shiitake Flavor against Platelet Aggregation." *Biofactors* 22, no. 1–4 (2004): 177–179.

Shodhganga, 2011. Go to Shodhganga.inflibnet.ac.in:8080/jspui/bitstream/.../09_chapter%201.pdf.

Sigler, L., J. R. Bartley, D. H. Parr, and A. J. Morris. "Maxillary Sinusitis Caused by Medusoid Form of *Schizophyllum commune*." *Journal of Clinical Microbiology* 37, no. 10 (1999): 3395–3398.

Sliva, Daniel. "Medicinal Mushroom *Phellinus linteus* as an Alternative Cancer Therapy." *Experimental and Therapeutic Medicone* 1, no. 3 (2010): 407–411.

Smirnou, D., M. Krcmar, and E. Prochazkova. "Chitin-Glucan Complex Production by *Schizophyllum commune* Submerged Cultivation." *Polish Journal of Microbiology* 60, no. 3 (2011): 223–228.

Stachowiak, B., and Regula, J. (2012). "Health Promoting Potential of Edible Macromycetes under Special Consideration of Polysaccharides—a Review." *European Food Research and Technology*. (Impact Factor) 234(3).

Stamets, Paul. "Chaga, the Clinker Fungus: This Mushroom Looks Scary But Can Benefit Health." Last updated December 25, 2015. huffingtonpost.com/paul-stamets/chaga-mushroom_b_1974571.html.

Stamets, Paul. "Lion's Mane: A Mushroom That Improves Your Memory and Mood?" Last updated October 8, 2010. huffingtonpost.com/paul-stamets/mushroom-memory_b_1725583.html.

Stamets, Paul. "Antipox Properties of *Fomitopsis offinalis* . . . Agarokon from the Pacific Northwest of North America." *International Journal of Medicinal Mushrooms* no. 3 (2005).

Steady Health. "Matsutake Mushroom—Health Benefits." Last modified October 15, 2010. ic.steadyhealth.com/matsutake_mushrooms_health_benefits.html.

Suehiro, M., N. Katoh, and S. Kishimoto. "Cheilitis Due to *Agraicus blazei* Mushroom Extract." *Contact Dermatitis* 56, no. 5 (2007): 293–294.

Takahashi, A., T. Endo, and S. Nozoe. "Repandiol, a New Cytotoxic Diepoxide from the Mushrooms *Hydnum repandum* and *H. repandum* var. *album*." *Chemical & Pharmaceutical Bulletin*, 40, no. 12 (1992): 3180–3184.

Tateno, H., H. C. Winter, and I. J. Goldstein. "Cloning, Expression in *Escherichia coli* and Characterization of the Recombinant Neu5Acß2,6Galß1,4GlcNAc-specific High-Affinity Lectin and Its Mutants from the Mushroom *Polyporus squamosus.*" *Biochemical Journal* 382, part 2 (September 1, 2004): 667–675.

Tobert, J. "Lovastatin and Beyond: The History of HMG_CoA Reductase Inhibitors." Nature Reviews Drug Discovery 2 (July 2003): 517–526.

Torkelson, C. J., et al. "Phase 1 Clinical Trial of *Trametes versicolor* in Women with Breast Cancer." *ISNR Oncology* 2012 (January 2012).

Turkoglu, Duru, et al. "Antioxidant and Antimicrobial Activities of *Laetiporus sulphureus.*" Food Chemistry, 2007. Find abstract on Elsevier.

Wang, G., et al. "Systemic Treatment with Vanadium Absorbed by *Coprinus comatus* Promotes Femoral Fracture Healing in Streptozotocin-Diabetic Rats." *Biological Trace Element Research* 151, no. 3 (2012): 424–433.

Wang, H., J. Gao, and T. B. Ng. "A New Lectin with Highly Potent Antihepatoma and Antisarcoma Activities, the Oyster Mushroom *Pleurotus ostreatus.*" *Biochemical and Biophysical Research Communications* 275, no. 3 (2000): 810–816.

Yamasaki, A., et al. "A Protein-Bound Polysaccharide, PSK, Enhances Tumor Suppression Induced by Docetaxel in a Gastric Cancer Xenograft Model." *Anticancer Research* 29, no. 3 (2009): 843–850.

Yang, M. M., Z. Chen, and J. S. Kwok. "The Anti-tumor Effect of a Small Polypeptide from *Coriolus versicolor.*" *American Journal of Chinese Research* 20, no. 3–4 (1992): 221–232.

Yang, Newman, Schulik. (2011). Patent US20110189220. www.google.com/patents/US20110189220.

Yuan, Z., P. He, J. Cui, and H. Takeuchi. "Hypoglycemic Effect of Water-Soluble Polysaccharide from *Auricularia auricula-judae* Quel. on Genetically Diabetic KK-Ay Mice." *Bioscience, Biotechnology, and Biochemistry* 62, no. 10 (1998): 1898–1903.

For Yukiguni research go to: www.yukigunimaitake.com/inthenews/Index-kb2.html.

INDEX

wholly chanterelle, 32–33
winter chanterelle, 26–27
chicken of the woods *(Laetiporus gilbertsonii),* xiii, 2, 5–7
clinker polypore. *See* chagas *(Inonotus obliquus)*
clitocybes, 131, 134
cloud mushroom. *See* maitake *(Grifola frondosa)*
Cole, Bill, 145
Columbia River Gorge, xiii
compass, xi
conifer bear's head *(Hericium abietis),* 35, 36–38
coral fungi, xviii, 85–90
   crown coral, 89–90
   spring coral, yellow coral, 87–88
Cortinarius species, 121, 122, 131, 136
   See also wood blewit *(Clitocybe nuda)*
cremini. *See* portobello *(Agaricus bisporus)*
crown coral *(Artomyces pyxidata),* 85, 86, 89–90

D
dancing mushroom. *See* maitake *(Grifola frondosa)*
devil's snuff. *See* gem puffball *(Lycoperdon perlatum)*
Devil's urn *(Urnula craterium),* 24
   See also black trumpets *(Craterellus species 01)*
Douglas fir, xx, 59

E
ear fungus. *See* fan-shaped jelly fungus *(Dacryopinax spathularia)*
eburiko. *See* Fomitopsidaceae *(Laricifomes officinalis)*

enokitake *(Flammulina velutipes),* 137, 142
entolomas, 121
   See also Cortinarius species

F
fairy ring mushroom *(Marasmius oreades),* 124–25
false morels *(Gyromitra species),* 73, 75, 76, 78
   See also morels *(Morchella brunnea)*
fan-shaped jelly fungus *(Dacryopinax spathularia),* 80, 84
field guides, xvi
floccosus *(Hydnellum suaveolens),* 35, 45–46
Fomitopsidaceae *(Laricifomes officinalis),* 2, 14–15
foraging
   permits and limits on, xi
   safety tips for, xi–xii
fried chicken mushroom *(Lyophyllum decastes),* 114, 115–17

G
Galerina marginata. See honey mushroom *(Armillaria ostoyae)*
gelatinous mushrooms. *See* jelly fungi
gem puffball *(Lycoperdon perlatum),* 63, 68–69
giant puffball *(Calvatia gigantea),* 63, 66–67
gilled mushrooms, xviii, 94–108
   Agaricaceae, 126, 127–30
   fairy ring mushroom, 124–25
   honey mushrooms, 105–6
   Lactarius species, 109–13
   mica cap, 103–4
   oyster mushrooms, 98–102
   russulales, 107–8
   shaggy mane, 96–97

mica cap *(Coprinellus micaceus)*, 103–4
morels *(Morchella brunnea)*, xi, xiv, xviii, 72–78, 137
   finding, xvi, xx
   season for, xiii
Mount Adams, xiii
Mount Baker Wilderness, xiii
Mount Rainier, xiii
Mount St. Helens, xiii
mushrooms
   boletes, 47–61
   books on, 146
   chanterelles, 18–33
   cleaning, storing, processing, xv
   coral fungi, 85–90
   cultivated, 137–43
   gathering, xvi–xxi
   inedible, toxic, hallucinogenic, 131–36
   jelly fungi, 79–84
   kits for growing, 144
   lobster, 91–93
   morels, 72–78
   other resources for, 145–46
   polypores, 1–17
   prints of spores, xvii
   puff balls, 62–71
   tooth funghi, 34–46
   Tricholomataceae, 114–23
   See also gilled mushrooms, *specific varieties of*
Mushrooms Demystified (Arora), 146
Mushrooms of the Pacific Northwest (Trudell & Ammirati), 16
mycenas, xiii, xx

N

National Audubon Society Field Guide to North American Mushrooms (Lincoff), 146

Native American land, foraging on, xi
Neah Bay, xiii
North Cascades, xiii
Northwest reishi *(Ganoderma oregonense)*, 12–13, 137

O

Ocean City (WA), xiii
Ocean Park (WA), xiii
Olympic National Park, xiii
orange-latex milky. *See* saffron milkcap *(Lactarius deliciosus)*
oyster mushrooms *(Pleurotus populinus)*, xix, 95, 98–102, 137
   finding, xiii, xvi, xx
   processing, xv

P

Pacific Crest Trail, xiv
Pacific golden chanterelle *(C. formosus)*, 19, 20–22
pear-shaped puffball *(Morganella pyriformis)*, 63, 70–71
Personal Location Beacons, xii
pholiotas, 131, 135
pig's ear *(Gomphus clavatus)*, 19, 30–31
pine mushroom. *See* matsutake *(Tricholoma magnivelare)*
pink bottom. *See* meadow mushroom *(Agaricus campestris)*
pleurotaceae family. *See* oyster mushrooms *(Pleurotus populinus)*
poison puffball *(Scleroderma citrinum)*, 71
polypores, xi, xviii, xix, 1–17
   artist's conk, 3–4
   black trumpets, 23–25
   cauliflower fungus, 16–17
   chicken of the woods, 5–7

ABOUT THE AUTHOR

Jim Meuninck is a biologist and counselor who has, for more than forty years, studied the use of wild plants and mushrooms as food and medicine in North America, Europe, Central America, Japan, Mexico, and China. He coauthored the FalconGuide *Basic Illustrated Medicinal Plants* with his daughter, anthropologist Dr. Rebecca Meuninck. He has seven field guides with the FalconGuide imprint. He also authored the Kindle book *What Is a Meaningful Life*.